ROAD TO WELLNESS

A Beginner's Guide on Your Path Toward Optimal Health

ROAD TO WELLNESS

A Beginner's Guide on Your Path Toward Optimal Health

Dr. Jacey Folkers

YouSpeakIt
PUBLISHING
*The Easy Way
to Get Your Book
Done Right* ™

www.YouSpeakItPublishing.com

I want to dedicate this book to the hope for a healthier and happier community. To all those who take initiative to improve their health and the health of those they love.

Beloved, I pray that you may prosper in all things and be in health, just as your soul prospers.
~3 John 1:2

Acknowledgments

Where to begin?

So many people have helped bring this book to life through their presence, wisdom, guidance, and ability to let their light shine.

My rock, my love, my biggest supporter on a daily basis: my wife, Carrie. For always allowing me to pursue my goals and my purpose in life.

My kids: Mandy, Kali, Kiara, Skylie, Avy, and Shiloh; for teaching me about living life in the moment.

My sister, Andrea, who has always been my steadfast supporter.

My brother, Kyland, who has helped me become the person that I am today simply by being himself. Being only eighteen months apart, we've shared countless experiences and have much understanding of each other.

My parents, for always being there for me, even today, in every aspect.

My friend, Dr. Omar Anguiano, with whom I've shared many struggles and successes, from rooming together in graduate school to now, each running our own clinics.

My mentors: Dr. Charles Webb, Dr. Datis Kharrazian, Dr. Joseph Mercola, Dr. Ron Grisanti, Dr. Daniel Pompa, Dr. John Bergman, and many more; from whom I have learned so much about true health and the importance of educating patients to bring forth healthy lives.

My patients. You know who you are. Thank you for allowing me to be a part of your world. I hope to help grow and expand the health potential in each of you and of those you love.

Contents

CHAPTER FIVE

Introduction

This book will help you adopt a healthier lifestyle. I talk about the ideal mindset shift needed to start understanding what health is and how to begin moving toward your optimal health.

I discuss the effects of stress and how important it is for us to understand what stress — especially chronic stress — does to our health. Stress can have major effects on brain health and almost every chronic condition. It's important to figure out if your stress is contributing to some of the health problems you may be experiencing.

In the book, I discuss the process of developing a leaky gut and how a leaky gut can lead to many health problems. It's sometimes difficult to see the connection between the state of your gut health and the negative effects on your health. It should not be overlooked.

I also discuss how important it is to be active and to make exercise a priority. We are meant to move and need to move on a daily basis. I discuss better ways to address stress, gut health, nutrition, and fitness. All these things need to be considered to improve your health and have the life you want.

I wrote this book to reach more people. I have dedicated many years of my life to educating and teaching others about ways to improve their health. Sometimes I feel I can't reach enough people from the confines of the offices that I practice in.

In my many years of practice, I've treated countless patients with health problems brought on by stress, gut problems, poor diet, and poor lifestyle. While we were growing up and going to school, there wasn't a class that taught us how to be healthy.

I didn't learn how to properly manage stress while growing up, or how to heal my gut and keep it healthy. I had to learn these things on my own, later in life, from other experts in those areas.

I want to be able to share this priceless information with everyone who needs it. Even though you don't live in the same town I practice in, I want to be able to share with you the important pieces to focus on to begin improving your health and your life.

If you can identify which area you feel you struggle with most—stress, gut health, lack of exercise, or poor diet—then you can go straight to that topic's chapter to start reading. Chapter Two talks about stress. Chapter Three focuses on gut health. Chapter Four talks about the importance of exercise.

You can go straight to Chapter Five and start to implement the recommendations, such as the various foods to focus on or avoid and the specific supplements to help with stress and its effects. Feel free to go straight to the chapter that focuses on your area of struggle.

If you do have the time, I highly recommend you read from beginning to end. I think Chapter One will help you shift into the mindset to begin to take control of your health. I believe that since you are reading this book, that process has started, and you are already making — or are about to make — changes to improve your lifestyle and your health.

I sincerely hope everyone who reads this book gains the confidence and desire to begin to change and improve their health. I hope this book serves as a stepping-stone to help you begin the journey down your path to wellness.

I purposely didn't go into great scientific detail or expand too much on all the topics included, but I am giving you the key points and areas to focus on. You can start implementing these ideas today. There is no reason to wait to begin changing bad habits. There is no reason to continue to eat poorly or to continue to cheat yourself out of the benefits of exercise.

I hope this book inspires you to focus on one of the most important gifts you've been given — your health. The fact is you have more control over your health than anyone else, including any doctor.

Everything you have done up until this very moment has contributed to your current state of health. What you decide to do from this point on will determine whether your health worsens or improves.

You are the CEO of your health. Use this book to lead you to a happier and healthier destination.

CHAPTER ONE

What Wellness Really Means

YOUR DEFINITION OF HEALTH

While growing up, I witnessed a lot of my extended family — aunts, uncles, and grandparents — experience poor health. I also witnessed how the system they used to deal with their poor health did not work well for them. Either they ended up succumbing to more complications or losing their fight to a disease such as cancer.

After seeing this, I learned a lot. I decided to dedicate my life to educating myself about a new path, a new way of thinking about wellness: preventative healthcare. This education involved alternatives to medications and surgery, as well as recognizing the fact that lifestyle greatly impacts our health.

This approach has worked for my family and me. I have two daughters who have autoimmune conditions, as does my wife, and we have been able to manage those conditions through natural methods. It is something that I think the rest of the world also needs to be aware of, to embrace, and to experience. What we do can greatly influence our health.

It's Not the Lack of Disease or Symptoms

What does the word *health* mean to you?

How would you define *health* for your friends or family?

Webster's definition says health is "The state of being free from illness or injury."

Does that sound like your definition of health?

If it does, you are not alone. Many of the patients I have had the privilege of treating over the years define health similarly.

It's a common belief that if a patient has not been diagnosed with a condition, or they are not experiencing symptoms, that means they are healthy. What can be problematic is when that same person believes their health issues are resolved when, upon being diagnosed with a condition, he or she takes medications, has surgery, or both.

Do you define health by just how you look or feel? The way you define health will affect the things that you do. Those things can then ultimately optimize your health or hinder it.

Many people are convinced that getting sick or staying well is greatly based on family history, genetics, or what medications or surgeries they have access to. They may not realize that how they live impacts their health much more. Many people still believe that their health is greatly determined by their genetics, and that it can't be changed, regardless of how they live their lives.

In reality, the greatest impact on your health and wellness is your belief system. Your belief system about health will affect your approach to maintaining or improving your health.

I want you to ask yourself:

What do I believe determines my health?

The World Health Organization defined health in 1948 as, "a state of complete physical, mental, and social wellbeing and not the absence of disease or infirmity."[1]

There are many definitions of health, but the most important one is the one you believe because your definition will ultimately reflect how healthy you can and will be.

---

1   who.int/bulletin/archives/80(12)981.pdf

The first step is to pay attention and be aware of your belief toward health. The next step is to be conscious about what you do to promote health in your life. You almost always find these two things are congruent with one another.

Health Is Not Just About How You Feel

How you feel, of course, is important, but feelings can be subjective. How you perceive something can change the way you feel, even at a physical level. People have different perceptions and levels of pain and discomfort; it varies from person to person. But being healthy can't be defined entirely by how you feel.

For example, a few years ago I was vacationing in Maui, and I witnessed a man who appeared to be healthy while on his honeymoon on the beach. Suddenly, out of nowhere, he suffered a fatal heart attack. Moments before this, he was relaxing with his new bride, and there was no indication of what was to come. There had been no warning sign.

Unfortunately, as humans, we can't always go by how we feel. We need to take a proactive approach to promote health continuously and to prevent these things from happening.

Every cell in your body is programmed to express your health potential. You have about seventy-five to one hundred trillion cells. Once you start to compromise the health of your cells, you begin to compromise the health of your entire system. This is not something you can always feel.

Most diseases develop through a process that can't be felt until the later stages. You cannot feel your arteries slowly becoming clogged, or cancerous tumors growing, or autoimmune diseases attacking your tissues. The symptoms usually surface once the disease has taken hold and much tissue damage and destruction have occurred.

By providing your cells with what they need on a regular basis, removing toxins that can compromise their function, you can help prevent and, in some cases, reverse these disease processes.

Symptoms are warning signs that your cells, tissues, or system as a whole has something going wrong. There are usually two primary causes of system malfunction: either something is missing, or something is interfering with your ability to function optimally. Both these factors can be present simultaneously, and often are.

Most pharmaceutical medications only mask these symptoms or warning signs and allow these disease processes to continue.

Are your cells moving away from optimal health potential?

These symptoms, as well as other unpleasant or questionable physical reactions are indicators:

- Tiredness
- Digestive problems
- Irritability
- Lack of focus
- Aches
- Pains
- Inflammations

Lab Values and Medications

One of my favorite places to visit in my youth was Colorado, where there was such great beauty in the mountains and the forest. I grew up in Nebraska, where there are no mountains, so I greatly admired the picturesque peaks and the beautiful nature. It was awe-inspiring for me. What amazed me the most was the interaction of all the components: the mountains, streams, plants, trees, animals, insects, all these different pieces working together in an amazing ecosystem.

As humans, we often forget that we are part of that ecosystem. Humans have drifted from nature in both physical and mental capacities. We no longer seem to believe that we are part of nature or governed by the same natural laws.

Imagine for a second you are watching a herd of 170,000 caribou. The caribou make their annual migration 1,600 miles south during the fall. Imagine that you suddenly see people feeding 130,000 of these caribou prescription drugs during their migration.

Would that seem strange to you?

Would you ask yourself why on earth people are giving these animals drugs?

If you are thinking that these animals don't need drugs, it's a normal, natural way to think.

But aren't humans animals, too?

The over-usage of medications in America is staggering. A couple of years ago, I heard that Americans consume about twenty-five million pills per hour, every day. Yet, millions still die every year of chronic diseases.

The normal approach that most Americans take when it comes to their health is visiting a doctor when they don't feel well. The doctors will perform an exam and perhaps order some labs. If they find certain markers out of range, they often will prescribe medications. Sometimes medications are prescribed without labs, simply based on the symptoms expressed by the patient.

The drug will change the outcome of the lab value by either raising or lowering the marker that was out of range.

Was the cause ever really determined for that patient's complaint?

In most cases, the cause of whatever symptoms that are being treated are not usually due to the lack of a particular medication. In other words, people don't develop a headache because there is a lack of Tylenol in their system.

Since humans are animals, too, why is it acceptable for 70 percent of Americans to regularly take prescription drugs that are not addressing the real issue?[2]

WHAT HEALTH REALLY IS

After practicing for over fifteen years, I've come to realize a lot of people don't grasp the real concept of health. For a lot of people, as I mentioned earlier,

2   newsnetwork.mayoclinic.org/discussion/nearly-7-in-10-americans-take-prescription-drugs-mayo-clinic-olmsted-medical-center-find/

they believe if they haven't been told they have XYZ condition, they are healthy.

If you are not prioritizing your health, putting it as a top priority, you may not achieve what you want in your life. Poor health significantly decreases your overall potential. You can't be the spouse, significant other, parent, grandparent, son, daughter, sibling or friend if you don't understand what health is and are not making it a priority to move toward it.

The Definition of Wellness

Your ideas and beliefs about health influence what you do—how you move, how you eat, and the decisions that you make. Many people believe genetics is the biggest contributing factor when it comes to long-term health; however, our environment and lifestyle play an even more significant role.

The remaining factors are based on lifestyle and the choices that we make. These lifestyle factors contribute to how our genes will be expressed and how healthy our cells will be. Once you decide to accept that what you do, how you think, and the decisions you make have significant impact on your health, you can start moving away from diminishing health and sickness and move toward optimal health.

You can adopt a wellness mindset, and that will allow you to move toward health.

What is wellness?

We hear the term used in different ways. The basic definition is "the state or condition of being in good physical and mental health."[3] As I previously mentioned, the World Health Organization defined health and wellness as "a complete physical, mental, and social wellbeing, not merely the absence of disease and infirmity."[4] The two most important components of each of those definitions, and the most essential, are physical and mental health.

Wellness is a dynamic act of progress, change, and growth. To dispel the belief that wellness is more than being free of illness, you must change your mindset. Become aware of the different choices and begin to make the right choices toward a healthy and fulfilling life.

It's important to stress the notion that wellness is not the absence of disease, but the presence of conscious, self-directed, and evolving processes working toward

---

3   Saswati, Jenna, and Namita Mohanty. "Understanding Mental Health of Adolescents" *Indian Journal of Health and Well-Being* 6(10). Indian Association of Health, Research, and Welfare: 968.
4   who.int/bulletin/archives/80(12)981.pdf

achieving your full potential. The process of wellness can't fully begin until you understand that your well-being is related to everything you do and every emotion you feel.

It's not just genetics, luck, or chance; it's the cyclical aspect of what you do that contributes to your wellness. In turn, your wellness then directly affects your actions and emotions. It's an ongoing cycle.

Being Aware of Your Current State of Health

The cycle of wellness can continue to feed itself positively or negatively. In making the right lifestyle choices, your wellness will improve. The healthier you become, the more prone you are to continue to make healthier choices and have healthier behaviors.

If you have the mindset that what you do does not really matter, or maybe you think it matters but you haven't really gotten around to doing much about it, then your wellness will suffer. Poor lifestyle choices will cause you to move away from wellness and continue to perpetuate that movement until you are stuck making those poor choices.

Despite all the information that many Americans have, they still do not believe that lifestyle choices can impact their overall wellness. As a result, the number of Americans suffering from or dying of chronic illness is significant. By the time we start to realize that what we do matters, it may be too late. Procrastination with our health is a huge problem. Many of us put off our health and wait until obvious signs are present that reveal we are no longer healthy, but very sick or dying.

It is important to be aware of your current state of health. By this, I do not mean paying attention to how you feel. Pay attention to what you do on a day-to-day basis.

Take the time to answer these questions:

- Do you feel you are participating in healthy behaviors?
- Are you thinking healthy thoughts?
- Are you choosing to eat foods that provide nutrition and vitality?

Make a list of the things you are doing that you believe are providing wellness. Also, make a list of the things you know are *not* optimizing your wellness potential. Be aware of what you are doing and what effect it is having on your health.

Now, answer these questions:

- Are you taking medication?
- What are you taking those medications for?

- What do you think precipitated that condition that prompted this medication to end up in your cabinet?

Why are animals in the wild not taking medications for chronic metabolic conditions like we humans do? Why are we not giving the caribou I mentioned earlier pills every day?

You need to become aware of where your current lifestyle actions and environment are taking you. Wild animals don't need medications as they do not typically suffer with the chronic metabolic diseases we humans do. They live in the environment they are supposed to, and if the environment doesn't suit them, they change their environment. They go to where they can continue to thrive. It goes against natural law to try to manipulate their physiology with drugs. We are ultimately changing our physiology with many of the medications we take.

Part of being aware of our health is recognizing the impact of the external factors, namely, *stress*. Stress is experienced daily, and it is because our environment is putting incredible stress on our physiology. Think of humans as a species. We are animals — not wild animals — but we are animals. Most of us in the United States are animals trapped in cages that we call cities. That in and of itself is a constant stress for humans.

When deciding between medication and lifestyle changes, most people will think short-term versus long-term. Medication is often chosen because of immediate effects. I often say that drugs are merely bandages on problems. By adopting healthy behaviors and choices, you not only improve your well-being but also provide a positive mindset for coping with the stresses of life.

Finding Your Why

In a Forbes article entitled, "Know Your Why," Margie Warrell points out that, "Unlike animals that are driven mainly to survive, we humans crave more out of life than mere survival." She goes on to say that when our reason for survival is ambiguous and unclear, "we can quickly fall into disillusionment, distraction, or a sense of quiet despair. . . . There is an alarming increase in the rate of drug and alcohol abuse, depression, and suicide along with a growing reliance on anti-depression medications. . . ."[5]

This all seems to indicate that many people are questioning the reasons for survival or longevity.

Do you know what you want out of your life, what is most important to you?

---

5   Warrell, Margie. "Do You Know Your 'Why'? 4 Questions to Find Your Purpose." Oct. 30, 2013. Search forbes.com for "sites margie warrell 2013".

What is your *why* for doing what you do?

When you want to make your health top priority, you need to have a why.

What can you achieve or strive for if you do not have your health?

You might know clear as day what your why is.

What gets you out of bed each day, driving you to do what you do?

I can tell when a person knows what their why is by a certain look they have in their eyes. When someone knows why, they have that look of determination, focus, and passion. They behave in ways that reflect their purpose and drive.

What gives your life purpose?

A common saying is:

People who don't stand for something can easily fall for anything.

Living with purpose means focusing on things that matter to you. Another wise saying we hear often is: *The things that matter most are rarely things.*

We often fail to realize that we all have other people watching us: what we do, how we live. These people could be kids, grandkids, siblings, nieces, nephews, significant others, spouses, parents, friends, or people you don't know personally.

People may be looking to you as an example. People depend on you. For me, my whys are my family and being a health practitioner. I would not be able to be the role model I need to be for my family or patients if I did not make health a priority.

What is important to you?

What do you want most in life?

You can have that which is most important to you, but you must realize there is a purpose bigger than you. Working toward optimal wellness will assist you in following your life's purpose. Knowing your why and being powered by a clear purpose are starting points for a wellness lifestyle. There is little you cannot do when you know your why, and, when you do know, your health almost always becomes a priority.

THE COMPONENTS OF WELLNESS

When people come into our office, they often don't know where to start. Prior to coming to our clinic, they may have purchased a program online or from an infomercial, such as a workout program, a diet program, or a coaching program. Frequently, they start out fine, but they don't get the result they want so they quit or they simply don't finish the program. Mostly, that is because there is no real system in place that helps them navigate the program in an easy-to-follow fashion.

Understanding the components of wellness and how to go through them is important. That's why I want to share this book so people can understand there is a way and a system available that allows them to navigate this process so they can achieve the goals they desire.

Deciding to Take Action

Humans are motivated to move toward pleasure and away from pain. Both pleasure and pain come in a variety of forms: physical, yes, but also emotional and mental. Most people are genetically and culturally driven to move away from pain and toward pleasure. You can relate to this, I'm sure.

If you had a job that was unbearable, you most likely made a change in employment to alleviate that pain. Perhaps your reflection in the mirror reminded you that you are not as physically fit as you once were. This may lead you to start going for walks or to a gym.

In both examples, the main motivating factor is moving away from pain. Pain can really motivate us to make a life change. We need to be careful with this, though, because until we experience suffering of some kind in certain areas, we can end up painting ourselves into a corner, especially when it comes to health.

Some people put off their health for years or decades leading to a tremendous amount of damage to their health. This makes it much more difficult to reverse the negative repercussions of their own unhealthy behaviors.

We can also move toward pleasure with our decisions in life. We need to be careful how we do this also because we can confuse pleasurable circumstances with pleasurable moments. What I mean is we can make decisions for immediate gratification without being conscious of the potential long-term negative effects.

Let's say you desire some fresh-baked cookies after dinner. This is a way for you to gain pleasure, not avoid pain. It will give you some immediate pleasure. It's okay to make choices that bring you pleasure, but if you decide to eat cookies every day after dinner, that could become a problem and create negative repercussions.

Whether you are moving toward pleasure or away from pain, it's important to consider the long-term effects of your decision. Everything you do has short-term and long-term effects, both good and bad. These effects accumulate over time.

Where are you in life right now?

Largely, your situation is a result of your prior decisions. You may find it easy to blame others for your difficulties. But, the truth is that positive thoughts and actions bring forth positive rewards, just as negative thoughts and actions often lead to negative results.

I don't have a crystal ball, but I promise you that if you want to have a healthy future, you must start today:

- Make good decisions.
- Think healthy thoughts.
- Make responsible choices.

Your life and your health will thank you for it.

Breaking Old Habits

There is no denying it. We are creatures of habit. We have become slaves to our habits. They can become inhibitors, and some have the power to control our lives. Many habits can prevent us from having the health we strive for. James Clear, author of the article "Transform Your Habits," reminds us that bad habits interrupt your life, prevent you from accomplishing your goals, and jeopardize your health. He explains that most bad habits are formed in response to two conditions. Most often we develop them as a way of dealing with stress, or as a way of dealing with boredom.[6]

According to scientists at the University College of London, it takes sixty-six days to break a bad habit and replace it with a new, healthier behavior.[7]

It doesn't have to be that way, though. You can learn new, healthy ways of dealing with stress and boredom, which can then take the place of your bad habits.

First, you must realize that habits, good and bad, play a role in your life. Some behaviors will provide benefits while others can be used as coping mechanisms. Some of the benefits we get from certain behaviors can still cause us harm, such as the biological cravings experienced due to tobacco or drug addiction. Another example is the emotional benefit we gain from staying in a bad relationship.

If you're coping with stress, the habit may manifest in the form of clenching your jaw, biting your nails, or tapping your foot. Since bad habits do provide some benefit in your life — in the sense that they may help you cope — it may be difficult to eliminate them. You need to replace a bad habit with a new habit that provides a healthier way of dealing with stress. You need to work

---

6   jamesclear.com/how-to-break-a-bad-habit
7   ucl.ac.uk/news

to change any bad habit that may be keeping you from improving your health.

Let's say you decide to begin to replace your habit of watching TV and eating potato chips with exercising and eating vegetables. As your self-image improves, you will gain more self-respect and discipline. This, in turn, can then create a desire to take on more challenges and set new goals in life. Then, you gain more confidence. Instead of streaming movies online before bed, you can read a book. Maybe instead of drinking soda, you switch to drinking water.

This new confidence fosters a new habit of expressing your positive energy toward others. If your energy is positive, you can attract and influence the people in your life to also take control of their lives and follow your lead. All these benefits are a product of the simple decision you made to change your old habits of watching TV and eating potato chips.

The decision to change your bad habit might not only benefit you, but it may also positively impact others in your life.

The Five Pillars of Optimal Health

It's important to recognize that what you do greatly contributes to how healthy you are now and in the future. Once you believe this to be true, and once you decide you want to make changes and begin breaking old habits, you can start down your road to wellness.

This road can lead you to amazing places and opportunities you may have thought were not possible for you. Your imagination is your best attribute right now because what you imagine and envision today can become a reality tomorrow. Once you decide to take the road to wellness, your potential becomes boundless.

In my practice, I begin by focusing on five key components of wellness. I call them the five pillars of optimal health.

They are:

1. Nervous system health and the capacity to release stress
2. Hormonal balance and the health of your organs
3. Detoxification to reduce toxic stress
4. Nutrition
5. Fitness, motion, exercise

I will expound further on these five pillars throughout this book. You may be familiar with pillars four and five and understand that exercise and nutrition can bring about excellent results. I want you to know how to implement all these pillars because, while you can get decent results from the application of a couple of them, you will get the optimal results you want when you put them all into practice.

You know you have much to live for and others who count on you. You know you have things in life you want to experience and new challenges you wish to take on. You owe it to yourself and your family to begin to incorporate wellness practices in your life.

Are you ready to unleash your personal wellness potential?

If so, let's start down the road to wellness together.

CHAPTER TWO

———————————

Stress and How It Impacts Your Life

SOURCES OF STRESS

One of the main ways we determine our potential to be healthy and well is our ability to cope with stress. Stress means different things to different people. What causes tremendous stress for you can be of little concern to another person. Additionally, some people are better equipped to handle stress than others. But, ultimately, what we do to contribute to our health and wellness helps us handle the effects of stress.

Stress is the body's reaction to various stimuli, and the stimuli can be real or perceived. When you feel some type of threat, a chemical reaction will occur in your body as a way to self-protect. This reaction is called *fight-or-flight,* or the *stress response*. When this happens, your heart rate goes up, your breathing quickens, your muscles tighten, your blood pressure rises, and your digestion slows.

This stress response is a survival mechanism, and we all have it. It is a powerful and necessary thing. Our bodies are designed to hold small doses of stress. However, what prevents us from being as healthy as we want to be is long-term chronic stress that we tend to have in our lives.

That is why we talk about the impact of stress on our lives and health.

Physical, Chemical, Emotional, and Environmental Stressors

Studies show that the average high school student today has the same level of stress as a psychiatric patient in the early 1950s.[8] Stress is at an all-time high. Stressors are all around us and come in many different forms. It's important to understand these different forms to know what you can do to reduce the effects of stress on your health.

When most people think about what stress is, they think of emotional stress. Emotional stress can take a

---

8   psychologytoday.com/blog/anxiety-files/200804/how-big-problem-is-anxiety

serious toll on your health, but there are other forms you need to be aware of.

The main three stressors are:

- Physical
- Chemical
- Emotional

Physical Stress

Those are physical traumas, like a slip or a fall, a car accident, a sports injury, or some other repetitive activity. Poor posture can be a physical stress causing imbalances throughout the body; even poor mechanics when doing a physical activity may not be ergonomically ideal. This can cause physical stress.

Additionally, using equipment that is too cumbersome can put stress on the body. If you are out of shape or lacking physical fitness, that can put stress on your body. Being overweight will necessitate your body to work harder to do everyday tasks, so that increases the stress on your body as well.

Chemical Stress

Chemical stressors include:

- Poor nutrition
- Smoking
- Using alcohol or drugs

There can be many chemical stressors in the water you drink, the food you eat, and the air you breathe. Personal care products can be contributing stressors. It's important to understand that anything you ingest that is not a nutrient, your body works to process and tries to eliminate. That becomes a stress.

Emotional Stress

This can be devastating for many. The loss of a loved one can cause incredible amounts of stress on someone and their health. Emotional stress is magnified by how we perceive any particular event. Life can be difficult. How you respond to stressful events is what makes all the difference.

Do you feel powerless, or do you take control of your actions?

You can get into a negative thinking habit that can cause you to feel unhappy and become more stressed. These negative emotions can be programmed into your brain causing you to have a negative thought process automatically.

There are ways to create new neural pathways and break these negative thinking habits to minimize the effects of emotional stress. I recommend being cautious of your thoughts and making an effort to focus on the good things in your life. No matter what is going on, things are not always as bad as we can make them seem at times.

Identifying Your Major Health Stressors

It's common knowledge that stress makes people sick. It's not always easy to apply this knowledge to yourself or your health problems. We don't always recognize the patterns easily because there is often that lag time between the source of stress and the occurrence of a symptom or disease, which comes later.

To help you identify what is impacting your health, ask yourself:

What was the most stressful period of my life?

Did this period coincide with a year or two of any health problems that I experienced?

The answers to these questions may not be the health problem you are struggling with today, but the stress you endured could be the trigger that led to those early health issues which may also have led to your current health struggles.

Stress comes in many forms. We have an area in our brain called the *hypothalamus,* which senses when a stressor is present. This is when an alarm is set off in your body. Nerves and hormones tell your adrenal glands, located on top of your kidneys, to release a surge of hormones, including adrenaline and cortisol.

Adrenaline is what increases your heart rate, elevates your blood pressure, and boosts energy supplies. *Cortisol* is the primary stress hormone that increases the sugar in the bloodstream, enhances your brain's use of glucose, and increases the availability of substances that help repair tissues. It prepares you to fight or take flight.

Cortisol will also help functions that are necessary for that fight-or-flight situation. Your immune system becomes depressed, your digestion slows, and your reproductive system and growth processes become suppressed.

This stress process also communicates with regions of your brain that control mood, motivation, and fear. The whole process is designed to only last temporarily. Once the perceived threat has passed, hormone levels return to normal. Adrenaline and cortisol levels drop, and your heart rate and blood pressure return to normal. Systems in the body resume their regular activities.

A problem arises when stressors are always present and that fight-or-flight reaction stays turned on. This chronic long-term activation of the stress-response system with constant output of cortisol and other stress hormones can disrupt all your body's processes.

The very system that is supposed to save you ends up causing much damage to your health.

This chronic stress creates an increased risk for several health problems, including:

- Anxiety
- Depression
- Digestive problems
- Heart attacks
- Insomnia
- Weight gain
- Hormone imbalances
- Headaches
- Memory impairment
- Autoimmune diseases
- Cancer

The Cumulative Effect of These Stressors

Stress is like a bucket filling up over time. As the bucket fills and fills with more stress, our health can start to drop off. Our nutrition may go south, we may stop making time to exercise, and when we are stressed, we usually don't set time aside for rest or recovery.

I recall when my youngest daughter was very sick in the hospital. I was so stressed over her condition that I hardly slept, ate, or did anything else for several days. When I did finally eat, I chose junk food from the hospital cafeteria. I recall a big slice of cake and a soda were items in one of the first meals I chose at the time. I recall feeling so depleted and emotionally drained. That big slice of cake just looked so good. What I did, however, was put more stress on my system. I ended up feeling even worse after eating it because of the increased demands on my body to now process all the sugar, fat, and other unhealthy things in that cake and soda.

This was not the ideal way for me to help my body during a highly stressful time. My stress bucket was overflowing, and I should have chosen better, more nutritious foods. I also should have tried to go a for a walk or even a quick workout. It's important to try to balance out stress with things we know are good for us.

Many of us have stress that just goes on and on and continues to rise over time. That bucket is getting filled to the rim. It's like a full glass of water. If you just barely move the glass, the water spills over the rim. But, if you do things to keep that stress from getting too high, you can keep that water level lower in that glass. Now, you can move it around and even shake it a little bit without spilling it.

So, when we decide to do things to better manage stress, we can continue to function better and not allow the stress to negatively affect our health.

It's important to continue to make wise decisions about our health, especially during times of stress. Often, stress is not completely in our control, but what we do during times of stress is within our control. I made a mistake by eating an unhealthy meal when I was extremely stressed, and I paid the price by feeling even worse after.

Continue to eat nutritious foods and try to include some form of exercise when you are under stress. This will help prevent you from adding more unnecessary stress to your life.

Lifestyle has so much influence on how stress affects our health. The better we take care of ourselves through good lifestyle choices, the better we can handle stress and prevent our stress bucket from overflowing and causing health problems.

THE EFFECTS OF STRESS ON YOUR HORMONES

Hormones control pretty much every process of the body. Stress is something that impacts your body in good ways and bad ways. When chronic stress persists and is unresolved, it can affect hormones and create imbalances that change all kinds of physiological processes — digestion, mood, energy levels, and the ability to focus and get things done. We want to be aware of how stress impacts our hormones and how hormones impact our overall function, health, and life.

Cortisol

I mentioned earlier the little part of your brain called the hypothalamus that controls stress. There is a sophisticated process by which your brain, when perceiving a threat, releases hormones to help the body's ability to stay and fight or flee the scene.

This process is known as the *HPA axis*, and the result is the production of cortisol. It serves like a bucket brigade at a fire. One person hands a bucket of water to the next in a line, bucket after bucket, person after person, to put out the fire.

Cortisol is necessary for our survival. Without it, we could not react. It is often expended with physical activity, like the kind you'd need if you were being chased by a bear. Cortisol affects many activities within our bodies without our conscious involvement. Chances are when you see an attacking bear advancing toward you, you won't stop to debate possible reactions and outcomes. Your sympathetic nervous system will kick in, and the cortisol will function to prioritize responses for survival.

These cortisol effects are necessary to help you deal with stress. They provide the body with the energy necessary to survive. Cortisol has anti-inflammatory properties to help the body control inflammation. It can counteract bronchial stress, remove and prevent swelling from insect bites, or help inflammation from a sprained joint. It can prevent eyes from swelling shut due to allergies.

Without our conscious involvement, cortisol affects:

- Energy required for movement to fight or flee
- What information you perceive via your senses: smells, sights, sounds, and so on
- How you make decisions
- Metabolism
- Immune system
- Blood flow

- Insulin sensitivity
- The stimulation of healing properties for potential wounds

The kind of stress you experience most often, however, probably does not rate the same as an angry bear coming to attack you. Common stressors now are more about non-life-threatening problems. Our bodies still prepare for the worst. This can lead to an excess of cortisol, or too much cortisol coursing through your body at the wrong time. For instance, you may be stressed about a work situation when you're trying to get to sleep at night. Cortisol is not your friend at that point!

High levels of cortisol influence cells that participate in the body's immune reaction, especially white blood cells, natural killer cells, monocytes, macrophages, and mast cells. This is done to focus more energy on the task of survival. Cortisol will also contract the mid-sized arteries in the body to force more blood and energy to the working muscles. All this is done to help you survive the stress while it is present.

However, most stress today doesn't require us to use our muscles to flee or our energy to fight. We release much cortisol into our bodies without the physical releases — such as running — that our body was designed for.

An excess of cortisol also has the following effects:

- Depresses the immune system
- Decreases function of major organs and systems, such as digestion, elimination, and reproduction
- Inhibits growth and collagen formation
- Negatively impacts protein synthesis
- Stops bone formation

When too much cortisol is produced over an extended period of time, all these effects can lead to things like weight gain, extra hair growth, irregular menses, loss of muscle, depression, and insomnia. Eventually, this high cortisol output can start to burn itself out when stress stays for too long. This can lead to a situation where your body can no longer produce the necessary cortisol to help you handle stress.

When the body is no longer able to produce the correct amount of cortisol, this is called *adrenal exhaustion.* Some practitioners also refer to this as *adrenal fatigue syndrome.* This can lead to more breakdowns of health, which we will soon discuss.

The Problem With Prolonged Stress

Stress is almost impossible to avoid. You are equipped to handle and survive most stressors. But stress can be a perception, and how you perceive things can magnify the amount of stress your body feels it's under. When the stressors last for longer periods of time, they can have devastating effects on your health.

Have you ever had that *gut feeling* or experienced a nervous stomach?

Science has shown over time how chronic stress can wreak havoc on your gut and your digestive health. I will discuss this topic further in the next chapter, but I want to outline how stress impacts your gut. Much of your overall health begins with the gut, so it's important for you to understand this concept.

Cortisol does decrease digestion like we have mentioned, but it also has harmful effects on the tissues of your gastrointestinal (GI) tract. It breaks down the protective mucosa of the gut. It decreases nutrient absorption and oxygenation, as well as inhibits blood flow to your digestive system as much as four times, which leads to decreased metabolism. Cortisol also significantly decreases enzyme output in your gut which can decrease the availability of important nutrients.

Stress results in many alterations to your body, especially your gut.

This will lead to many GI disorders, including:

- Inflammatory bowel disease
- Irritable bowel syndrome
- Peptic ulcers
- Acid reflux
- Food allergies

It will lead to other GI diseases, and ultimately many other system diseases.

Hippocrates once said all diseases begin in the gut. It's well known that stress is a trigger for many chronic conditions to occur. Stress can be detrimental to your health, including damaging your gut.

Harvard researchers explained psychology combined with physical factors caused pain and other bowel syndromes.[9] Psychosocial factors influence the acute physiology of the gut, as well as other symptoms. The brain can influence the stomach directly — for example, when we think of eating or see a delicious food commercial. This activity can cause a release of the stomach's digestive juices without food being there. Mental stressors can also send signals to the gut which can cause pain and other GI symptoms.

---

9   health.harvard.edu/diseases-and-conditions/the-gut-brain-connection

In other words, stress such as depression or other psychological factors can affect the movement and other functions of the GI tract, cause inflammation, or make you more susceptible to infections.

The connection goes both ways. Troubled intestines can send signals to the brain, just as a troubled brain can send signals to the gut. Therefore, a person's stomach or intestinal distress can be the cause of anxiety, stress, or depression. The brain and the gastrointestinal system are so intimately connected that they should be viewed as one system.

Long-term and short-term stresses can affect your gut health in many ways. As this stress affects your gut, your declining gut can then cause you more stress, so it can become a vicious cycle, ultimately ruining your overall health.

Hormonal Imbalance

I don't want to get too technical about the finite details of all the hormones that are affected by stress, but I do want to address the main ones as stress does involve many hormones, and hormones are what conduct this amazing symphony that occurs in our body.

The main hormones that play a role in stress are:

- Cortisol

- DHEA
- Testosterone
- Estrogen
- Progesterone

Thyroid hormones are also impacted by the effects of stress. Thyroid hormones are important for helping regulate many important bodily functions, but I want to go over cortisol once again and what it does.

In its normal rhythm, cortisol is ideally at its highest level around 8:00 a.m. Afterward, it gradually declines throughout the day. Occasional spikes do occur, particularly when the body is stressed. In a healthy individual, levels are usually lowest between midnight and 4:00 a.m., at which point they begin to rise again.

When adrenal fatigue occurs, there can be a change in this normal pattern or rhythm. When this happens, other hormonal changes also occur. Eventually, continued unresolved stress will cause cortisol to rise to such a high level that the adrenal gland becomes exhausted and its production begins to drop. DHEA production begins to decrease. DHEA is the precursor of testosterone, estrogen, and other critical steroid hormones. When its production drops, it affects the levels of those other hormones.

Testosterone is a hormone that is produced in both men and women. A decline in testosterone is associated with a decreased sex drive and libido in both sexes.

Estrogen and *progesterone* are two main sex hormones in women. They are produced in men also, but in different quantities. Estrogen and progesterone work in sync with each other. They oppose each other in their actions and work as checks and balances to achieve hormonal harmony. These hormones are produced in the ovaries but are also made in the adrenal glands in both sexes.

During stress, and especially adrenal fatigue, progesterone production is reduced. When this happens, estrogen dominance occurs. Estrogen dominance has numerous adverse effects, such as fibrocystic breast changes, disturbances in blood sugar, fertility, and uterine fibroids.

Estrogen dominance in women is most often evidenced by:

- Swelling of the fingers, more noticeable on fingers wearing rings
- Irritability and cramps before menses
- Irregular periods
- Fluid retention
- Foggy thinking
- Depression
- Fatigue

Estrogen dominance can increase thyroid-binding proteins in the blood, resulting in hypothyroidism. Estrogen dominance also worsens adrenal function, which in turn aggravates and causes more estrogen dominance. In addition to the high estrogen causing hypothyroidism, the adrenal fatigue itself also lowers thyroid function. Then the lowered thyroid function, in turn, worsens adrenal fatigue. Many times, patients are treated for hypothyroidism when the underlying problem is, in fact, adrenal fatigue.

These are some of the main hormone changes and imbalances that can occur with adrenal exhaustion, which is brought on by chronic stress. These are the underlying imbalances that are the common denominator for a variety of problems. There can be different expressions of the same illness affecting different organs and body systems, but most of them can be linked to adrenal exhaustion and how that changes when unbalanced.

THE EFFECTS OF STRESS ON YOUR BRAIN

I find the human brain quite fascinating. It is capable of pretty incredible feats, visible now through advanced technology. Just think of all the amazing discoveries that have come to fruition that started out as someone's thought. I am still amazed at how airplanes fly and can carry thousands of people all over the world. The potential of the human brain is quite limitless.

In treating so many patients over the years, I have seen the effects of stress and how that can create diminishing potential in people's brains. The human brain is composed of one hundred billion neurons plus one trillion glial cells. We actually have more brain cells as a newborn than at any other time in life. From the minute we are born, we go through a slow degenerative process of our brain.

It is important to calm stress and deal with its effects in order to slow this process because, quite frankly, you are not really stuck with the brain that you have today; you can actually work at improving it.

Normal Brain Function

We can't remember much of our first years of life because the area of the brain called the hippocampus was not developed enough to build a rich memory of events. Science says that you have about 70,000 thoughts every single day.[10] Those thoughts contribute to who you are and what drives you.

10 observer.com/2017/05/you-have-70000-thoughts-every-single-day-dont-waste-them-decision-making-process/

It is important to make an effort to have healthy and positive thoughts move through our brains to help maintain health and function. The brain is one of the heaviest organs in the body. It's the most oxygen-demanding organ, and it uses up to 30 percent of the body's glucose supply.

There are different areas or lobes of the brain that have different functions. The frontal lobe or cortex stretches between the temples. This is where most of our personality stems from. It governs impulse control, emotional drive, motivation, planning, and fine motor coordination.

The temporal lobes are on both sides of the brain above and behind the ears. They are responsible for hearing, speech, memory, emotional responses, and distinguishing smells. The hippocampus, which is the learning and memory area, is contained in this lobe. These lobes are for perceiving sensations like touch or pressure, and interpreting sensations such as texture, weight, shape, or size. The temporal lobes also help you become aware of your environment.

Our *cerebellum,* or *little brain,* is made up of two distinct lobes that sit at the back of your head directly above your neck. It calibrates muscle coordination and movement when you perform basic actions such as placing a fork to your mouth.

The occipital lobe is located in the back of the brain. It processes visual information such as recognizing shapes, color, and motion.

For optimal function, the neurons in the brain need to be receiving enough oxygen, glucose, and stimulation to function. Chronic stress and other conditions compromise function, as mentioned earlier. This can lead to improper or unhealthy neurotransmitter activity, which can and will promote brain degeneration.

If the brain is not functioning optimally, consider whether there are factors impeding it, such as:

- Blood sugar levels
- Inflammation
- Liver problems
- Hormone imbalances

The Brain Under Stress

Many people think the brain is its own isolated organ. The brain does communicate with the body and receive signals through the nervous system to then process and respond to those signals. The brain impacts and controls so many different things. It is also impacted significantly by the rest of your body.

Everything affects everything when it comes to health and wellness.

Did you know your brain and gastrointestinal system originally formed from the same tissue when you were in utero?

As I mentioned earlier in this chapter, your gut and your brain share a major connection. The health of your brain is therefore impacted by the health of your gut and vice versa. We will discuss this more in the next chapter.

Nothing is more damaging to the brain than stress. Stress can atrophy the brain, making it shrink. It promotes brain inflammation and upsets brain function. Stress can also cause a breakdown of the blood-brain barrier, allowing infectious agents in.

The stressors that take a devastating toll on your brain are the ones you are not always aware of. This is stress from chronically poor diet, lack of exercise, and marginal health. The most common way people damage their brains in this country is from blood sugar imbalances due to high-carbohydrate diets. The human body was not designed to process all the carbohydrates we consume.

Other stressors that contribute to brain degeneration include:

- Smoking
- Food intolerances

- Food allergies
- Anemia
- Bacterial infections
- Gut parasites
- Autoimmune diseases
- Joint pain and inflammation
- Poor digestion

After a while, these stressors worsen brain function.

As mentioned, stress causes increased cortisol. High cortisol will over-activate the hippocampus, which will cause it to falter in its functions. This can lead to insomnia or energy crashes during the day. This can also affect your memory and your ability to learn.

Stress impacts your brain's command over the autonomic nervous system, which regulates breathing, digestion, heartbeat, organ function, and more. When this system falters, people will experience conditions such as dry eyes and high blood pressure.

Stress affects the mid-brain, which is located at the top of the brain stem. This area deals with survival, mating, and emotions such as anger and love. Stress can overexcite the mid-brain, which can cause more stress. When the vicious cycle of stress aggravates the brain, brain inflammation is the outcome.

This is important because chronic inflammation in the brain not only can impair neurological function, but it also contributes to inflammation in the body, such as in the joints or the gut. This is most commonly seen in abdominal inflammation, which actually can have its roots in the brain. This inflammation and overstimulation of the mid-brain can create a cycle that causes more brain degeneration.

Another thing that chronic stress can cause is constriction of blood vessels that leads to poor circulation in the brain. All in all, stress, as you can see, is very damaging to the brain.

The Effects of Prolonged Stress on Your Brain

What happens when you have prolonged unresolved stress that has gone on for years and years?

This can cause a lot of damage to your brain. There are many different areas that can be affected when prolonged stress lingers on and on.

If someone has frontal lobe degeneration, for example, this would affect the areas that the frontal lobe controls, things like handwriting, which can get noticeably worse. General laziness or a lack of motivation is noticed. There could be episodes of inappropriate social behavior.

You may also find you are not as good as you used to be with doing things like crossword puzzles, math problems, or other cognitive tasks. These are all early signs that the frontal lobe is degenerating, brought on by prolonged stress.

The temporal lobe problems could show up in the form of poor memory, maybe forgetting why you walked into a room, where you parked your car, or where you put your car keys. Also, there is difficulty hearing with background noises and ongoing episodes of insomnia. These symptoms are concerning because these are the earliest signs of Alzheimer's disease.

Parietal lobe degeneration symptoms would include feeling unstable in darkness or with high-heeled shoes on; misjudging where your body is in relation to your environment, which causes you to bump into things more often; being unable to recognize objects through touch, and becoming more prone to falls, sprains, and strains.

If the cerebellum is affected, typical symptoms include becoming carsick more often and experiencing seasickness easily. Those whose cerebellums are affected may become nauseous from staring at wallpaper, someone's shirt, or rugs that have stripes or other complex patterns on them. Episodes of dizziness and vertigo are common. Poor balance is also an issue with people with cerebellum degeneration. Additionally, a subtle shake can occur at the end of a movement.

Occipital lobe degeneration will display symptoms such as difficulty processing visual information and recognizing shapes, colors, and motion. You may experience visual hallucinations, occasional flashes of light, or persistence of a visual image after it has been removed. Also, visual floaters could be present when this area is affected.

Prolonged chronic stress is quite damaging to your brain and your health. In adults, the symptoms I have mentioned usually mean there is degeneration affecting those specific areas of the brain. You may have some, or many, symptoms if your overall brain is not functioning well. If that is the case, recognize that you are having issues, and that your overall brain endurance is not at its optimal level.

My own personal story with stress includes running a busy practice — there is always stress with that. I also have six daughters, by the way. That is stressful in and of itself. One of my daughters is getting married soon. When we learned of the engagement, my wife and I assumed she would get married next year. However, we discovered it was going to be in September, which was only a few months after getting engaged.

As you know, weddings and the planning of weddings can be stressful. One of my daughters is twenty-one years old; she is a sweet, carefree soul. Most things in life come easily to her. So, now it is crunch time.

She has been texting me every day as the wedding approaches, "I need to talk about the dance," or, "When I walk down the aisle, I want this."

It's all fun, and I am very excited for her. I just want everything to be perfect for her on her wedding day.

I guess the moral of the story is that when you have a lot of daughters, stress is to be expected. Especially since you will likely end up helping each of them plan their special day.

We need to learn ways to avoid getting too worked up over most things in life. Instead, we should try to enjoy them!

CHAPTER THREE

Why Your Gut Health Is So Important

WHAT THE GUT ACTUALLY DOES

A lot of people don't value or fully understand the importance of the gut. I'll share a quick story about my experience with gut problems as a child growing up.

I was only four years old when I had my tonsils removed. I remember having frequent sore throats during my childhood. About four to five times a year, my throat would become very sore, it would hurt to swallow, and this discomfort seemed to last a long time. I was put on antibiotics many times for this.

I also remember, as a child, having chronic gut pain, stomachaches, headaches, and constipation. I often had a difficult time going to the bathroom.

I continued to deal with these digestive issues and headaches up until my late high school years. I was around eighteen years old when I was introduced to a probiotic. After taking probiotics for about a year, I realized the occurrence of a sore throat, headaches, and constipation had diminished. I actually felt normal.

Previously, I thought it was normal to have a sore throat, headaches, and constipation and to take over-the-counter medications to treat them. Since then, I realized that focusing on my gut was crucial to my health and overall immune function. As time progressed, I also started to make other conscious changes to my diet and lifestyle to improve my gut health.

Today, the health of the gut is a major area of focus with most of my patients.

The Anatomy of the Gut

The GI tract is more complex and vast than most people think. We have about thirty feet or so of intestines. Imagine a very long water hose in your backyard. That hose is wrapped up and twisted and packed into a small space, like the intestines in your abdominal area.

Things are happening in this long hose that makes up part of what we call the *digestive tract*. Digestion and nutrient absorption happen in the digestive tract. It's not smooth inside like a water hose is. There is a lot of surface area in the intestines. There are many little tiny folds and crevices and tiny projections, called *villi,* that significantly increase the surface area inside that hose. This increased surface area allows for functions of the digestive tract, like absorption of nutrients, to occur more optimally.

As foods and liquids move through and are broken down, various enzymes are also secreted in the gut to aid in the digestive process. The gut also acts as a protective barrier to not allow harmful things into the body. Those things that are not nutrients and are not supposed to be absorbed in the circulation eventually get eliminated from the body.

The *enteric nervous system,* or ENS, is able to control all aspects of digestion independently. The spinal cord could be severed, but still the digestive system could continue to operate on its own without needing signals from the brain. It contains the same neurotransmitters and chemicals as the brain. This allows the gut to operate on its own.

There are two dozen small brain proteins, called *neuropeptides,* in the gut, as well as major cells of the immune system. Approximately 96 percent of the body's serotonin is produced in the gut.

Serotonin plays a vital role in digestion. It helps stimulate the release of digestive enzymes in the intestine. Serotonin and other hormones in the gut communicate with the brain. This communication is often referred to as the *gut-brain connection*.

The gut not only helps digest food, but it is also a main line of defense in protection from harmful disease-causing agents.

The mucosal barrier in the gut keeps at bay certain disease-causing agents, such as:

- Bacteria
- Allergic foods
- Parasites
- Environmental toxins

Absorption and Protection

Our digestive system has a dual purpose. It is important for absorption of nutrients, but it also prevents potentially harmful things from getting into our circulatory system. Most absorption of carbohydrates, proteins, fats, and vitamins occurs in the small intestine. Some nutrient absorption does take place in the stomach, but the stomach's main job is to break apart the food we eat chemically and mechanically.

Once the food passes from our stomach, our small intestine then goes to war for us, deciding what things are safe and what things are not safe. It gives that stamp of approval, allowing the good things into our circulatory system. The increased surface area, because of the villi throughout the small intestine, helps the absorption of carbohydrates, proteins, fats, vitamins, and minerals.

We also have a barrier that lines the intestinal wall. The *mucosal barrier* helps prevent more harmful things from getting through the wall of the gut. None of the food that we eat is sterile, so it does contain bacteria, toxins, and chemicals. This mucosal barrier prevents these potentially damaging molecules from getting through. It provides a shield of protection from harmful things from the outside world. It's important for this barrier to be healthy and adequate.

If this barrier breaks down, it can allow unwanted things to get into our body. When it breaks down and things get through, this is known as *leaky gut syndrome*. The leaky gut can lead to food sensitivities, cause inflammation, and lead to autoimmune conditions. We will discuss leaky gut syndrome more in detail later in this chapter. But in addition, the mucosal barrier also has a significant number of friendly bacteria in the gut that needs to be present. These friendly bacteria also help with digestion and offer protection from harmful bacteria.

This is sort of like the Earth's ozone layer—a thin layer of ozone in the atmosphere that ends about fifty kilometers above the Earth. The ozone acts as a selective barrier, making sunlight available for photosynthesis while simultaneously preventing the sun's disease-causing ultraviolet light from penetrating the skin. The protective portion of the ozone layer screens out ultraviolet light.

There is another layer of important micro-organisms that are an important addition to the mucosal barrier. Just like the earth has the ozone layer, our intestinal wall has a layer of micro-organisms. There are billions of bacteria forming this layer that lines the gut, providing another selective barrier. This bacterial barrier will prevent harmful substances from entering the body while allowing necessary nutrients to be absorbed for our cells to use.

The Bacteria That Reside in Your Gut

We have approximately one hundred trillion bacteria in our digestive tract. This is approximately ten times the number of cells that we have in the rest of our body. We have so many bacteria that most of us are more of a bacterial colony than we are human. Most of the bacteria resides in the large intestine of our gut. These gut florae aren't just catching a free ride in our gut;

they do help us with many things. The friendly gut bugs help us digest food. They protect us from harmful pathogens. These bacteria provide us with essential nutrients, such as vitamins. They also help train our immune system. Most importantly, if something goes wrong with the gut flora, something can also go wrong with our health.

In our microbiome, there are a hundred times more genes than in the rest of the body. This creates an ecosystem in our gut. The ecosystem is different from person to person. It's sort like a fingerprint. No two individuals have the same ecosystem in their gut. The environment that exists in the gut can and does affect this ecosystem. The environment is influenced by the foods that we eat.

Scientists have discovered that more and more diseases are linked to disturbances in our gut flora:

- Diarrhea
- Diabetes
- Obesity
- Atherosclerosis
- Colitis
- Crohn's disease

Even autism has been associated with disturbed gut floras.

When we are born, our gut is sterile. The birth process is when a baby gets inoculated by the flora of the mother. This is an important part of the journey through the birth canal. Babies delivered via C-section are unfortunately deprived of this important inoculation.

Messing with the flora early in life can have serious consequences. Antibiotic use has been shown to have some potential health consequences, especially when used early in life.

The gut flora also influences behavior, brain function, and brain development. I see effects of the brain-gut connection in my office every day. I witness mood improvements with patients who improve their gut health and increase probiotic consumption and improve their diet. We have a lot of little friends in our gut, so we need never feel alone.

The gut microbiota that have evolved in humans throughout life appear to play a pivotal role in both health and disease. In a healthy state, the gut microbiome has a variety of positive functions, including energy recovery from metabolism in nondigestible components of food, protection from a pathogenic invasion, and modulation of the immune system.

Dysbiosis — an imbalance in the gut bacterial flora — in the gut microbiota is becoming recognized as a factor that interacts with one's metabolism and can play a very significant role in many pathological conditions.

WHAT CAUSES PROBLEMS IN THE GUT?

Adam was one of my best friends. We would often have lunch together, sometimes a couple of times a week. We would talk about business, family, life, and goals. We had plans to partner up and build an incredible wellness center together. We spent holidays and birthdays together with our families. We were good friends and had much in common.

Approximately three years ago, he was told he had colon cancer. Prior to this, when we met up for lunch, I often noticed he rarely ate vegetables. I asked him why he chose not to eat them. He said he just disliked vegetables. Maybe he started not liking vegetables as a kid, and, in his adult life, he decided not to eat them.

I recall he would frequently say he was tired; he often had dark circles under his eyes. It appeared to me that he didn't feel 100 percent often. Then the cancer diagnosis came, and everything hit at once. Man, I wish there was something I could have done with all the tools and education I have. He was one of my best friends. I often regret not insisting he eat better or recommending that he add a super greens supplement to his diet to get the nutrition he was missing from lack of vegetables.

Not a day goes by when I don't wish I could have done something to help prevent or improve his condition. He lost his battle with cancer. Ultimately, stress and the unhealthy state of his gut likely contributed to his cancer, which ended up costing him his life.

I honestly did not think he would lose his battle with cancer. He didn't seem to be overly sick when I saw him. I am still in shock. He passed away about two years ago. He was a good friend, and a great dad and husband. He left three young children and his wife. He will forever be missed.

Not one of us is immune to the effects of stress and poor gut health.

Stress

Have you ever noticed when you go on a vacation or take a break from work, or from all the demands in life, you start to feel better?

Countless patients have told tell me they feel much less heartburn, indigestion, or other symptoms when they took a vacation. This is most often because they have a significant reduction in stress. If you were running from an angry bear, you would be experiencing some major stress. Your body would go into a fight-or-flight stage. Digestion would no longer be the most important thing for survival in that moment.

Guess what?

Your body can't tell the difference if you are being chased by a bear or worried about finances or have a deadline you must meet for work. In essence, the stressors make our bodies think we are constantly running from that bear. This can take a serious toll on your health, especially your gut health. If you are not lowering your stressors, your body will begin to produce more and more cortisol. This cortisol will start to disrupt sleep, slow down digestion, and erode the mucosal barrier of the gut. We need this mucosal barrier for protection. The stomach lining needs to be protected by this mucosal barrier from its own stomach acid.

That is why stress often leads to stomach pain. The stress hormones can break down the lining, causing tiny holes to form. This can then allow undigested food particles and unwanted bacteria to get through the gut lining. This can overexcite the immune system, leading to potential food sensitivities. We often order a food sensitivity test in our office to help determine which foods a person may be reacting to because of this.

Stress can cause a decrease in an important nutrient, like the amino acid *L-glutamine*. When this nutrient gets too low, it can cause a weakness in the cells of the gut, causing more holes and more problems. Stress will cause changes in the gut bacteria. More bad bacteria will begin to grow, and fewer of the good bugs will. We tend to see an overgrowth in yeast with people with chronic stress. Stress will cause us to begin to lose nutrients like magnesium, zinc, and B vitamins. Zinc is important for the healthy gut and for gut healing. Stress will also decrease your actual immune cells in the gut, leading to increased potential infections.

Any type of stress can cause all these things to occur:

- Eating a poor diet
- Not getting enough sleep
- Overexercising
- Overworking
- Taking many medications

All these stressors, when they become chronic, have a huge impact on the health of your gut and your overall health. We need to practice ways to reduce our stress.

Poor Diet

Diet is one of the leading influences on the health of our gut. It is ideal to have a variety of different strains of bacteria for a healthy gut. We can help influence the balance of our microbiome by paying attention to what we eat. Foods high in dietary fiber, like fruits, vegetables, nuts, legumes, and seeds, are the best fuel for gut bacteria.

When our good bacteria digest the fiber we eat, they produce short-chain fatty acids. These fatty acids help nourish our gut barrier and improve immune function. They also help prevent inflammation, which reduces the risk of cancer. The more fiber you ingest, the more your digestive bacteria colonizes in your gut.

There was a study done in 2015.[11] Researchers looked at exchanging the diets of African-Americans — high in fat and meat, low in fiber — with the diets of rural South Africans — high in fiber. After just two weeks of the rural South Africans following the high-fat, low-fiber Western-style diet, they had increased inflammation of the colon as well as a decreased production of butyrate. *Butyrate* is that short-chain fatty acid that is thought to help lower the risk of colon cancer. The African-American group showed improved gut health as shown on colonoscopy and measured by epithelial cell staining with decreased inflammation while following a high-fiber, low-fat diet.

When we eat low-fiber, processed foods, this deprives the good bacteria fuel it needs. This essentially starves

---

11   ncbi.nlm.nih.gov/pmc/articles/PMC4415091/

them until they die off. Foods high in sugar and more processed foods do correlate with a decrease in gut bacteria diversity. The bacteria can start to feed on our own mucosal barrier.

Some foods that contain antioxidants—like fruits, vegetables, red wine, and dark chocolate—can help increase the diversity of the gut bacteria. This is a good thing. I encourage patients to consume more lacto-fermented foods also. This is a good way to help introduce more probiotics into the gut. We teach people how to make their own sauerkraut, kombucha tea, and coconut yogurt. Eating more live-fermented foods is a great way to add more friendly bacteria to your gut. Adding more fiber-rich whole foods and fermented foods is one of the best ways to go.

Start significantly reducing processed high-sugar foods because they really aren't real foods; they are more or less packaged *food-like* substances. They won't provide fuel for your gut microbes, and they won't provide much benefit for you, either.

Antibiotics and NSAIDs

Antibiotics can be life-saving. They definitely serve a purpose when they are used appropriately, especially in emergency situations. Antibiotics have been used way too much for things they can't help, like viruses, for example. Antibiotics do destroy both good and bad bacteria in the gut. When the bad bugs come back, they tend to overpopulate the gut terrain, so the person who took the antibiotic has an overgrowth of bad bugs. They will often have too much yeast overgrowth as well. This will begin to disrupt the normal gut function. It can also weaken the immune system.

If you must take an antibiotic, it is important to eat a diet that is low in sugar and high in fiber. I also recommend taking probiotics as well as eating prebiotic foods to help provide fuel for the probiotics. Prebiotic foods are foods like onions, garlic, and sweet potatoes. These foods help fertilize the probiotics.

Antibiotics are like atomic bombs for the gut. They destroy everything, so it's important to replenish the gut microbiome. It is also necessary to repair the cells of the gut after taking antibiotics. I recommend taking L-glutamine, omega-3 fatty acids, zinc, and digestive enzymes.

Another set of harmful drugs for the gut are nonsteroidal anti-inflammatory drugs, or NSAIDs. There are studies that show how NSAIDs increase intestinal permeability. Holes are formed in the gut, allowing things to permeate through the gut that normally should not be allowed through. The use of these NSAIDs can also increase the risk of ulcers and intestinal bleeding. One study in particular, from *Neurogastroenterology and Motility* in 2012, found that as little as one dose of aspirin at 600 milligrams was enough to increase intestinal permeability.[12]

Like antibiotics, NSAIDs will cause disruption and change your gut bacteria. There was another study that showed how people who took NSAIDs on a regular basis had significant differences in the composition of their gut microbiome. "The bacteria composition of the gut varied with the type of NSAID ingested."[13]

These medications are overused in the United States. Approximately 15,000 people die per year as a result of aspirin and other NSAIDs.[14] NSAIDs damage the gut, and it's no wonder we are seeing more and more Americans diagnosed with autoimmune diseases, which are becoming epidemic. We need to use these types of drugs more sparingly, especially reducing the amount of frequency they are given to children. They simply cause too much damage to the gut and our overall health.

12   ncbi.nlm.nih.gov/pubmed/22757650
13   clinicalmicrobiologyandinfection.com/article/S1198-743X(15)00902-7/
14   phend.co.za/health/Nsaid.htm

WHAT HAPPENS WHEN THERE IS A BREAK-DOWN IN GUT HEALTH?

One of my daughters is ten years old. When we lived in California, we would go to the beach, and then traditionally we would stop for ice cream on our way home. At the time, my daughter was two and a half or three, so she would not be denied ice cream. The drive home was about an hour. During the last half-hour of the drive, my wife and I wanted to kill ourselves because our daughter would scream at the top of her lungs like she was crawling out of her skin. We could not understand why.

We soon realized that whenever she consumed sugar or gluten, it would affect her drastically. So, we decided to cut it out of her diet. That is when I started to give my daughter probiotics at a young age, and it made a significant difference in not just her attitude, but in her overall health. It was a night-and-day difference.

I prescribe probiotics to my adult patients. We see big differences between when one's gut is not healthy and when they start to make changes to improve it and prevent the breakdown. It is an ongoing, constant, everyday process that you need to work at. But the work is well worth it.

When that same daughter was in first grade, they thought she had a learning disability. We found out that she was eating sugar and bread at the school lunch. Once again, we put her on probiotics and had her eating better. She went from having difficulty learning and concentrating to being a straight-A student.

Malabsorption

We have all heard the saying: *You are what you eat.*

The human body is amazing, breaking down foods into their smallest particles and then using them to keep everything working. The digestive system can break down a piece of carrot, for example, and use that to make a liver cell function.

Our bodies really do pretty incredible things. But sometimes the saying *You are what you eat* isn't entirely true. Sometimes there can be a breakdown of some sort, and we are not absorbing much of those things that we put into our mouths. A more accurate saying would be: *You are what you **digest**.*

Imagine you took your car to one of those automated car washes. This car wash is going to take your car through several different stages in the wash. It rinses off your car, washes off the dirt, adds soap, uses more water along with spinning brushes to clean your car, rinses off again, maybe adds some wax, and finally it will dry your car. The whole process is well designed, and in the end, you have a nice, clean car.

But let's say the car wash has some sort of malfunction. Let's say it took your car through the car wash way too fast. When your car came out, it still had dirt and soap on it. It wasn't very clean at all. This is what can happen in your digestive system.

The foods you eat can move through your GI tract too quickly and not get absorbed into the body very well. There can be some sort of breakdown in the gut, like not enough enzyme production, to break down nutrients. There can be holes in the gut lining, and the cells of the gut won't work properly to break down things small enough. There can be inflammation and erosion in the gut wall. This will not allow nutrients to be absorbed. So, often foods can pass through our digestive system and never really make it into the bloodstream, where they can be used.

There can be several causes for this to happen in our digestive system.

More common causes are:

- Chronic inflammation in the intestine from an infection like a bacteria or parasite
- Leaky gut
- Celiac's disease
- Crohn's disease
- Prolonged use of antibiotics or NSAIDs
- Lactose intolerance and other food sensitivities

- Trouble with the liver, gallbladder, or pancreas
- Surgery
- Trauma
- Damage to the intestine

These are the most common causes I see, however, there are more things that can lead to malabsorption like birth defects or radiation therapies.

When these conditions exist, despite your best efforts to consume a wholesome diet, you may not be getting all the benefits from that good diet. Nutrients get passed through without being used. Your car wash just isn't working properly with all the proper stages needed.

Dysbiosis

Intestinal dysbiosis occurs when bad bugs in the gut begin to take over. Remember we have more bacteria in our gut than we do cells in the rest of our body. There are approximately four pounds of bacteria in the digestive tract. We need to make efforts to keep the colony of our gut happy and not allow it to be taken over by the bad bugs. Dysbiosis is significant and should be considered as a mechanism of disease in most patients.

This can be true for patients with conditions such as:

- Chronic gastroinflammation
- Autoimmune disorders

- Food allergies
- Food intolerances
- Breast or colon cancer
- Unexplained fatigue
- Malnutrition
- Neuropsychiatric symptoms

One useful test that can help identify dysbiosis is a comprehensive stool analysis. We work with a company that provides us with stool test kits. We can give or send this kit to patients so they can perform this test at home and send in to the lab for analysis. We can then get the results sent to our office and share this with the patient. This can help determine which bad bugs exist.

These bad bugs are known as opportunistic *pathogenic bacteria,* which means given the opportunity, these bacteria will proliferate and grow out of proportion compared to the beneficial bacteria. When this happens, there is a toxic byproduct or waste product that is produced from the bad bacteria. This starts to interfere with the beneficial function of the good bacteria. These toxins from the bad bacteria start to get into our circulation.

The bad bacteria negatively affect not only the gastrointestinal system, but also allow toxins to begin to accumulate in our body.

This creates a laundry list of symptoms, such as:

- Gas
- Bloating
- Diarrhea
- Constipation
- Skin conditions like eczema
- Psoriasis
- Hives
- Acne
- Fatigue
- Muscle and joint pains
- Brain fog

The toxins from the bad bacteria irritate the lining of your gut, and this leads to leaky gut syndrome, also known as *intestinal hyperpermeability*. This is when the protective barrier that keeps out the bad bacteria or larger-than-normal proteins breaks down. Now, the bad bacteria and larger molecules move from the gut into the blood. This can lead to system-wide inflammation. The bottom line is if the balance of good bacteria shifts in the wrong direction, it opens the door for opportunistic bacteria. Bacteria like *H pylori* can now wreak havoc on our bodies.

It's vital to eat a high-fiber healthy diet. It's also important to reduce toxin exposure and manage your stress. Many medications, especially antibiotics, can also lead to dysbiosis. Be aware of what is going on in your body and what effect it has on your microbiome. The bugs in our gut really do have a significant impact on our health. Make it a priority to keep the friendly bugs happy and not let them get pushed out of town and replaced by the bad bugs.

Leaky Gut

Leaky gut is a condition that can lead to more health problems than most realize. Gastrointestinal conditions, food sensitivities, and autoimmune conditions all can begin with leaky gut. This is why we put so much focus and emphasis on gut health in our clinic. You can begin to experience great health improvements by focusing on healing leaky gut.

The good news is leaky gut syndrome is treatable. One of the first things you need to do is cleanse the body of all the foods and substances that are causing the body irritation in the digestive tract. Then you need to spend time healing the gut. Nutrients such as essential fatty acids, vitamin C, vitamin B, L-glutamine, bone broth, probiotics, and more can help heal the gut.

If you really want to improve your overall health, you really need to start acting on this immediately. Especially if you have allergies, autoimmune disorders, or digestive disorders, you need to heal the gut.

CHAPTER FOUR

We Are Meant
to Be Physical Beings

WE ARE MEANT TO MOVE

In more than fifteen years of practicing chiropractic, I have seen the effects of sedentary living. I have physically touched and felt thousands of spines and extremities throughout the years. I can tell when a person is active or not by feeling and palpating their spine.

The more active individuals have more flexibility, more springiness, and more pliability to their spine. The more sedentary people have a spine that is more rigid, stiff, and sometimes like that of a steel rod. They typically have less bounce, and when I gently push against their spines, it has less spring compared to those of active individuals.

Regular motion keeps our bodies young. Active people have spines like that of children: springy and resilient. Active spines also adjust more easily.

Human beings are meant to move on a regular basis. According to an article in the *Annals of Internal Medicine*, prolonged sitting is associated with diminished health and increases in chronic disease.[15]

All the technological advances may have made us much lazier. We are adapting to our sedentary ways, but a lot of us are reaping the consequences of not moving our bodies.

Everything inside of our body is moving. Our heart beats, blood pumps, food digests, and cells divide — there is constant movement. The human body is a fascinating organism, which works and responds best when it is active. Movement is essential for our health.

The Active Lives of Children

Have you ever noticed how much energy kids seem to have?

My fourteen-month-old daughter can run, throwing her arms around recklessly, for a good amount of time and enjoys herself while doing so. Her movements

---

15   ncbi.nlm.nih.gov/pubmed/25599350

resemble that of a baby gorilla. In fact, we call her *Little Gorilla* because of this.

My three-year-old daughter is also very active and she regularly runs, plays, climbs, and jumps. She loves moving around as much as she can.

Then there are my two nephews who take being active to another level. If you could harness the energy that those two boys have and bottle it, you could probably power a small village because they can keep going for hours.

Children are meant to be active. In fact, it's very important for kids' development for them to move and be active.

It's also important for adults—we're just bigger kids, aren't we?

But, you might want to think twice about running around and flailing your arms like a gorilla because people might be a little freaked out. Or you may end up seeing yourself doing that online, posted by someone that secretly—or not so secretly—recorded your performance.

The problem today is that many kids are not able to have the activity that they need. Many kids are being diagnosed with attention-deficit hyperactivity disorder (ADHD), which often is not an accurate diagnosis. Physical activity is crucial for children and their development. We need to allow kids to play and move to express themselves.

Our bodies are designed to move. Movement is an expression of our minds. In fact, movement helps stimulate our mind in a very positive way. We have put so much focus on children sitting more during the days at school. There is much focus on academics. There seems to be less and less gym time or recess time in schools. Kids are spending more time sitting, using computers — not using books as much, but sitting and staring at the blue-light screens on computers or tablets.

There have been studies that have shown that kids who are more active get better grades. Activity is important, and when so much focus is on sitting and not moving, especially at a young age, this creates an imbalance. This imbalance can then carry on throughout life.

This can set these kids up for many future health problems:

- Obesity
- Diabetes
- Heart disease
- Autoimmune diseases

Other conditions can stem from this learned lack of being active. We have become too accustomed to being sedentary. Technology has not helped us in this area. We use technology well, and it has many benefits, but it seems to be taking a toll on our health.

Many of us work in jobs that don't require activity of our bodies, with the exception of simply sitting at a desk, clicking a mouse, and tapping a keyboard.

The narrative and relationship between our body and our movement are forgotten. We only notice our body when something goes wrong with it. We have in fact betrayed our bodies, ignoring and dishonoring them by using them purely as *hauling devices* to transport our heads.

Movement is crucial for development and healthy expression. We are meant to move from the day we are born.

Joint Range of Motion

It breaks my heart to think of all the years my mother has gone through physical pain because of problems with her knees. I recall at least four major surgical procedures she has had throughout the years and many other minor procedures. She has always had lots of pain and could never be very active because of it.

My mom obviously was not some retired NFL football player who had numerous surgeries to repair the years of damage she endured from the gridiron, but she did suffer from arthritis. Her doctor at the time, approximately thirty-five years ago, recommended surgery. That led to more surgeries. This all led to both knees being replaced with artificial knees.

Many Americans suffer from arthritis and joint pain. Every day, thousands of hips, knees, and other joint replacement surgeries occur in this country.

We have all heard the phrase: *Use it or lose it.* This is something we should take a little more seriously. We were meant to take our joints through regular movement and range of motion on a daily basis.

We have the innate need to stretch as soon as we wake up. This is because our bodies have been resting while we are sleeping; now it's time to get up and move. Stretch those joints to get ready to move around for the day.

Have you noticed how a cat spends time stretching every joint when it wakes up?

We need to be doing this also. Unfortunately, most of us do not move much more during the rest of the day.

Movement is critical for our overall health, including joint health, and it can help prevent and improve arthritis. Those who are dealing with regular joint pain and arthritis pain may not want to exercise because they are afraid exercise will make their pain and arthritis get worse. There is research that actually shows the opposite effect. Being active can improve joint function.

There was a Northwestern University study on 3,500 individuals in their fifties and sixties with arthritis.[16] They found that those individuals that got at least thirty minutes of exercise five days a week had a reduced chance of becoming disabled from their arthritis. In fact, the study showed improved function with a reduction in pain in those individuals getting regular consistent exercise.

This goes for all the joints in the body, not just hips and knees.

Your spine, which houses your spinal cord and nervous system, also needs movement. This is why chiropractic care is so important along with physical activity and exercise. Arthritic changes in the spine can not only cause neck and back pain, they can also negatively affect the *end organs* and body parts that those nerves innervate and supply.

Each vertebra in our spine has a nerve root that branches from that vertebral level in the spinal cord. That nerve root has branches of nerves that go to and

---

16   webmd.com/arthritis/news/20060106/exercise-prevents-arthritis-disability

control various organs that we refer to as an end organ. Lack of regular movement of your body, and especially your spine, can actually have negative effects on organ function. The vertebral bones and vertebral joints can lose their range of motion and function from a lack of regular motion. This can lead to arthritic changes in the spine, which can put pressure on those spinal nerves. When the nerves get pinched, this can choke off vital messages and signals to the organs they feed. Motion plays a huge role in our overall health, organ system function, and overall vitality.

Let's respect our bodies and spend time moving them to help them work, function better, and last longer.

Metabolism

Often, I hear patients say they just cannot lose weight like they used to be able to.

They say: *I think I have a slow metabolism.*

The term *metabolism* refers to the many processes in the body that occur when we convert food to energy. These processes also include eating, breathing, digestion, and energy usage to move nutrients throughout the body. This energy is also used to help rebuild tissues in our bodies and the elimination of waste from our bodies.

When a patient mentions the word *metabolism* to me, they are usually referring to the rate at which they are able to burn calories. They are assuming they are not able to burn calories at the same faster rate they once were able to. *Metabolic rate* is the rate at which we burn calories. There are differences between various individuals' metabolic rates. One person can seem to have a very fast metabolism and always stay skinny, and you may feel like yours is very slow.

Why is this, and what can lead to these differences?

There are many factors:

Age is one factor. A younger person who is growing and developing and hasn't reached adulthood can have a very fast metabolism.

Gender can be a factor. Most males have a faster metabolism than females.

A person's ***body size*** can lead to a larger metabolic demand.

Various ***hormones*** can affect our metabolism.

Caffeine and ***activity level*** can increase metabolic rate.

Pregnancy will affect metabolism.

A person's **overall body composition** will change metabolism. Body composition refers to the percent of body fat and percent of muscle that a person has. The more muscle mass they have, they'll have an increased metabolic rate.

Even a person's **body temperature** can influence their metabolism.

When you move more during the day through **exercise** or **routine daily movement,** like walking or standing, your body burns more calories.

Exercise has a significant impact on your metabolism.

When you participate in an activity that requires a lot of muscle activity, this is when your body is using the energy, called *glucose,* that is stored in those muscles:

- Running
- Lifting weights
- Kickboxing
- Dancing

These will all use energy to allow those muscles to work. That glucose that is used will also need to be replenished back into those working muscles. Both processes of glucose expenditure and glucose replenishment require energy to occur.

There are two main types of exercise:

1. Endurance — long duration, low intensity
2. Anaerobic — short bursts, high intensity

Both forms of exercise have benefits for overall health, but they each affect the body in different ways. The lower intensity endurance exercise will not have as much of a significant impact on our metabolism as the higher intensity, short duration exercise.

Here is why: The endurance cardio-style exercise will not burn up as much glucose in the working muscles and require as much glucose replenishment compared to the high intensity exercise. Things like weight lifting, sprinting, and other things done in short intense bursts will put more demands on the working muscles. This will require the body to use more energy to refuel those muscle groups. This will, in turn, put more metabolic demands on your body long after the exercise was completed.

Think of the body of an Olympic sprinter. They compete for only ten to twenty seconds or fewer in some events, yet they are very lean and have good muscle tone. They have high metabolic expenditures, which keep their bodies burning fat.

One great way to increase your metabolism is to start implementing some high-intensity or strength-training exercises in your routine.

THE IMPORTANCE OF EXERCISE

Most people think of exercise as a way to lose weight. It is, in fact, important and effective when trying to lose weight.

Exercise can help change the way our bodies look by improving muscle tone and reducing body fat. Besides weight loss and changing body composition, exercise also has many other positive benefits we should take advantage of.

These benefits include:

- Increased energy levels
- Improved immune function
- Reduced risk of many chronic diseases
- Improved mood
- Reduced stress
- Better sleep
- Improved libido
- Improved cognitive function
- Decreased likelihood of dementia

Weight loss should not be the only reason we decide to exercise.

As a general rule, everyone should aim for twenty to thirty minutes of some sort of daily physical activity, such as walking. If you haven't exercised for a very long time, not ever, or if you have a heart condition, arthritis, diabetes, or some other chronic health problem, please check with your doctor before starting an exercise program.

I recall a patient I treated more than fifteen years ago. She was a very sick woman. She had diabetes, arthritis, irritable bowel syndrome, chronic bronchitis, high blood pressure, brain fog, and very low energy. She was a former smoker. She took many medications for all the various symptoms and chronic pain she dealt with on a daily basis.

One thing I recall about her was how much younger she was than her husband. They were about fourteen years apart, and they had been married for about thirty-eight years. I was shocked the day her husband came in with her for one of her appointments. I was certain he was the younger one; he looked so much younger than she. He took no medications, had no aches or pains, had lots of energy, and appeared very youthful and fit. He was the older of the two; he was seventy-four years old. He really wanted his wife to get her health back.

The biggest difference between the two was that he exercised every day. She did not exercise at all. He told me he had an exercise routine he did every morning that included weight training and cardio. He had been doing exercise his entire life, he said. This man looked great for his age. It was evident his lifestyle habits and consistent exercise did wonders for his health and seemed to significantly slow the effects of aging. His wife, unfortunately, experienced the opposite effects from her various health conditions and lack of physical activity. She appeared much more tired and showed more of the effects of aging, though she was several years younger than her spouse.

The number of people in America over the age of sixty-five is on the rise. With this increase in an aging population, there is also an increasing number of people with brain and memory conditions like dementia. One thing that helps slow or prevent the cognitive decline that many older adults experience is regular exercise. One study showed how people who regularly exercise actually prevented brain shrinkage that occurred in a controlled group of people who didn't exercise.[17] This is incredible because we can interpret the results actually help not only our bodies, but also our brains stay young and function better by exercising.

According to the study, "We demonstrated that loss of hippocampal volume in late adulthood is not

17   umd.edu/news/news_story.php?id=7541

inevitable and can be reversed with moderate intensity exercise."[18] The *hippocampus* is a structure in the brain that is important and plays a significant role in our emotions, learning, and memory.

We all have heard of the benefits of exercise for our heart, fat burning, and increasing strength, but not many are aware how exercise can also impact our brain in so many positive ways. Our brain and nervous system is the master system of the body. This is what we really need to keep working on for as long as possible. A healthy brain promotes a healthy body and vice versa. Exercise slows down aging and contributes to longer living.

After working with the patient I mentioned above for about six months, we were able to get her off her medications. Her energy improved greatly. Her brain fog lifted. Her blood sugars were near perfect. She was no longer technically diabetic. She lost weight, and best of all, she was exercising with her husband. He was so ecstatic to have his wife back. They both stated that their marriage was more fulfilling than it ever had been before. I have had the privilege of experiencing many cases like this, but this one has always stuck in my head because of how young and healthy that man seemed and how that couple stuck together and did the work

_____

18   umd.edu/news/news_story.php?id=7541

to get her health back. He is the model of how I hope to be when I am in my seventies and beyond.

Finding the Type of Exercise That Is Right for You

Most Americans do not exercise enough. The American Heart Association recommends at least one hundred fifty minutes per week of moderate exercise or seventy-five minutes per week of vigorous exercise. You can also do a combination of both types, but less than 15 percent of Americans meet this recommendation each week.

Maybe a lot of people don't know which exercise is right for them.

I often hear, *I just do not have time to exercise;* but what I hear that person really saying is, *I just do not make time for exercise.*

Some of the busiest, most successful and productive people I know make it a priority to exercise. One of my friends and mentors, Dr. Charlie Webb, is a very busy man. He owns several companies, including a large consulting company. He teaches thousands of doctors and their staff members how to run successful practices. He is an author and has appeared on radio shows and TV commercials. He runs and operates his successful companies. He is also a husband and a father. I asked him once how he stays so productive and how he is able to stay on top of all the things he does day in and day out. He told me he always exercises. He always makes time for exercise to keep his energy up. This allows him to be more productive and get more out of each day.

We all have twenty-four hours in each day of our lives. It is not impossible for any of us to get the amount of exercise we need. Once we start doing it, it becomes easier and easier, sort of like brushing your teeth — just another part of your day.

I recommend you regularly add walking into your routine, if you haven't already done so. Twenty minutes of walking at least three days a week will do great things for your health. It's also beneficial to start higher intensity interval training. We refer to this as *HIIT exercise*. HIIT exercise is what will really start to transform your body composition. Fat burning and muscle toning will begin to be seen within a few weeks of doing consistent HIIT exercise programs.

Other benefits gained from regular exercise, as seen in many studies, include lower risk of these health challenges:

- Heart disease
- Stroke
- Blood clots

HIIT workouts also improve your cardiovascular system tremendously.

Don't think you should push yourself too hard for too long. Exercise is something you must adapt to. In the beginning, your body will tire easily and quickly. You shouldn't' push yourself to the point of exhaustion. I have some patients that cannot yet walk for a full twenty minutes. We encourage them to walk for ten minutes, or maybe less. As their bodies begin to adapt to the demands they are putting on it, they start to gain more and more tolerance for walking. Soon, they can go for fifteen minutes or more without tiring. Listen to your body. It's important not to overdo it.

Exercise is not all-or-nothing. If you don't regularly get in three or more workouts a week, you will benefit from some added exercise. When I don't have time available for a twenty- or thirty-minute workout, I will do a quick five-to-ten-minute high-intensity routine. This shorter burst-style workout can have great benefits. The way to do this also varies from person to person.

Your goal is to do a twenty- to thirty-second high-intensity burst. It raises your heart rate more than walking would. Then after twenty to thirty seconds, you rest for about one to two minutes. You then repeat this burst. I try to get four or five of these burst intervals on days I don't have the time to do a full twenty- to thirty-minute exercise session. This type of exercise really helps with fat burning and can be done almost anywhere.

Some of the movements I use for this include:

- Running up and down stairs
- Running in place
- Jumping rope
- Jumping jacks
- Mountain climbers
- Burpees
- Body squats
- Squat jumps
- Exercise bike
- Sprinting outside
- Rowing machine
- Elliptical machine
- Treadmill

I do like to change it up, and you can do anything you enjoy as a means to get your heart rate up. Sometimes I enjoy playing soccer with our daughters. Or, put on some music and dance with your kids to get the heart rate up. Change it up, and add some fun time in. But do make it a priority regularly to add physical activity into your days. Exercise can add fun and years to your life.

Exercise Detoxifies, Assimilates Nutrition, and Transforms Your Physique

Everything works better with regular exercise. Our body is always working to detoxify itself. Exercise and regular movement helps this process a great deal.

When we exercise, many processes help improve detoxification:

- Breathing increases
- Blood circulation is elevated
- Sweat forms on the body

Drinking lots of clean water assists with this process to move toxins out of the body. Exercise will stimulate your thirst for more clean water.

The movement of your body itself is also beneficial for the lymphatic and immune systems. The blood system has a heart that works as a pump to keep the blood moving throughout the body. The lymphatic system does not have a pump, and it requires movement to keep it circulating to cleanse and purify the body. We need to keep the lymphatic system moving, and regular exercise is what allows that to happen.

Exercise is great for reducing body fat. Toxins are stored in our body fat. As we lose more fat, those toxins will be eliminated. Our bodies hold onto fat as a buffer from toxins, so exercise is important to help remove both unwanted fat and the toxins it holds onto.

Digestion also will improve with exercise. Regular exercise helps stimulate movement of both the circulatory system and the digestive system. Many symptoms of poor digestion—like gas, bloating, and constipation—will improve with regular exercise.

Exercising and strength training can change your physique and make your body look more athletic and become stronger. This is one of the most common reasons many people work out. As you continue to exercise and incorporate more strength training, your body composition will change. I do recommend strength training for all ages and body types.

A lot of people still may have a misconception that weight training will make them bigger or bulkier. That is not true. The more muscle tissue you develop, the more efficient your body becomes at burning fat. Resistance training will also improve other things like bone density. It can help improve posture, range in motion, and function of your joints. Coordination and balance also improves with weight training.

Individuals who continue to do strength training are gaining many more benefits than just the increased muscle that they build and maintain. Building muscle does have its youthful benefits also. The more we move and work to stay strong, the more we stay young and live the way we want for a much longer time. Exercise to build muscle helps us detoxify from the many body systems it helps stimulate, but it will also help us look and feel more youthful, strong, and confident.

MAINTAINING PHYSICAL ACTIVITY

I feel fortunate to come from a physically active family. We all try to be active and push each other to continue to stay active and be as healthy as we can be. It just so happens that my dad has the world bench press record for his age and weight class.

My brother also holds power-lifting records and competes as a natural pro body builder. He plans to compete in the world natural bodybuilding competition next year. My dad and brother do weightlifting as a hobby and, as a result, maintain physical activity and exercise.

Exercise is necessary to participate in these types of competitions. You don't need a competition to exercise, but if you are a person who has a desire to compete, there are many ways to test yourself. These can be good motivational tools for many of us.

Not all people come from families that are physically active or are involved in athletics. No matter what a person's background is, whether you are a former Olympian or professional athlete, or if you have never been to the gym or owned a pair of running shoes, it is important to start being active and maintain some degree of physical activity.

Sometimes involving yourself in a competition can help motivate you to keep pushing. No matter what, you are always competing with yourself. Charting your progress and continuing to push yourself to reach new milestones is great, but never stop being active.

The Importance of Consistency

You will see the best results from changing your exercise level and diet when you are consistent. It takes time and effort to make exercise a consistent part of your life. I recommend people create a plan and have a concrete idea of what their workout schedule should look like. It doesn't have to be a complex program at all.

As I mentioned earlier, I recommend some people begin by walking three or four days a week for fifteen minutes. I recommend they figure out in their schedule which days work best for them. I like to recommend people try to do their exercise in the morning. It's one of the best times to exercise to help improve energy for the rest of the day. Sometimes, this may mean waking up a little bit earlier each day.

Putting this down on paper is a great way to start a consistent program. Creating a visual document to hold yourself accountable is a great way to start implementing your goals and your action plan. Put *exercise* on your calendar. View it as something that is as important as going to a doctor's appointment or meeting up with your Bible study group or going to your child's school event. You should make your exercise time a consistent and concrete time that has high priority. Whether it's a ten-minute or thirty-minute workout, you need to schedule it.

Of course, there will be days when other things get in the way and make it difficult to get in your scheduled exercise routine. Maybe your child gets sick and something unexpected comes up. But the important thing is to start to have consistency to gain momentum. Scheduling exercise as part of your day is a great way to get this going. Put it on paper and put it on your refrigerator so you see it every day. Hold yourself accountable and start doing this immediately. Your health depends on it.

A lot of people say they will start *on Monday*. Then many Mondays come and go. Or, in September they say they will start after the holidays. It's important for people to understand that part of consistency is starting. Once you get going, whether it's once, twice, or three times a week, at least you are rolling along. The biggest component is starting today, not waiting for the right Monday or the right January first to come.

Exercise Improves Your Brain Health

Most people begin exercising to help improve their body's overall appearance or to lose weight. It is one of the best ways to accomplish this. Exercise has many other positive effects on our health like lowering blood pressure, reducing risk of stroke, heart disease, and diabetes. It also can prevent and help with depression. Another benefit of exercise is its positive impact on our brains.

Exercise helps the memory center in the brain. Researchers say one new case of dementia is detected every four seconds globally. According to the World Health Organization (WHO), they estimate that by the year 2050, more than one hundred fifteen million people will have dementia worldwide.[19] So, start

---

19   who.int/features/factfiles/dementia/dementia_facts/en/
index2.html

exercising today, not just to improve your appearance or other body functions, but most importantly, to help improve your brain function. I see patients who have significantly less brain fog and improved memories after they have been sticking to a regular exercise program. One patient mentioned to me that she felt like her vocabulary had improved significantly since she had been exercising on a more regular basis.

Movement and exercise help our brain in many ways. We see improved memory, better mood, lower stress and anxiety, and improved sleep. There have been studies that show how exercise is associated with increase in volume of certain regions of the brain.

If you are physically capable of pushing yourself, then consider high-intensity exercises that really raise your heart rate, such as jump rope, jumping jacks, squat jumps, sprinting, rebounding (jumping on a trampoline), or any other type of high-intensity aerobic exercise. Just when you feel you can't go on, push yourself a little more.

The key is to find a way to boost your heart rate safely. Doing high-intensity interval training (HIIT) helps elevate something called *endothelial nitric oxide*. This is a chemical that helps dilate blood vessels, improves glucose uptake, and activates energy in the brain. This form of exercise is very beneficial for brain health.

Please use judgment when doing exercise so as not to do more harm than good. Sprinting around the block or doing squat jumps may be perfectly appropriate for one person while just increasing the walking pace may be enough for another.

Exercise Prevents Almost All Chronic Conditions

We have an epidemic in this country of many chronic health conditions.

These conditions are unique in that they are, for the most part, *earned conditions,* meaning they are mostly brought on from lifestyle habits:

- Cancer
- Heart disease
- Type 2 diabetes
- Obesity

These are diseases that are created from the way we eat and from the lack of exercise. Exercise is what we can use to help reduce the risk of these conditions and also help reverse them. Exercise is without a doubt one of the most powerful ways to help improve our health.

I can't state this enough: the problem is that so many Americans just don't move. Studies show how exercise has an anti-aging effect down to the cellular level. It helps keep your cells young and healthy.[20] You cannot become well unless you heal the cell. Exercise is that thing that helps heal our cells.

Whether or not you are overweight, exercise really needs to be a part of your lifestyle. Weight loss should not be the only reason you choose to work out. Exercise helps balance hormones in the body. One hormone in particular is insulin. Exercise will help improve your body's ability to regulate insulin. This is important on many levels. When insulin levels are more normalized, this will help with blood sugar levels so you will receive more health benefits. Insulin can be a very inflammatory hormone. Also, it can cause accelerated aging in individuals with chronically high insulin.

When insulin is properly regulated, it improves health in many ways:

- Increased energy
- Reduced pain
- Improved IQ and memory
- Better mood
- Improved immune function
- Slower aging

---

20   ucsf.edu/news/2013/09/108886/lifestyle-changes-may-lengthen-telomeres-measure-cell-aging

Exercise is one of the best medicines you can give yourself, and you don't have to go to any doctor to get it. You just start moving your body. Your body is meant for movement. It's the lack of movement that causes it to start to break down. We are adaptive creatures, so when we are sedentary, we are creating adaptations for sedentary bodies. The more sedentary we become, the more we adapt to being more sedentary. The most sedentary body I can think of is one that is no longer alive. Be more active, and be more alive.

Exercise is as important as sleeping and eating. Don't use your age or state of health to prevent you from starting your own exercise program. No matter your age, you will start to see enormous benefits for your health with exercise. Do not wait another day to get your exercise program started.

CHAPTER FIVE

How You Can Gain Wellness

LIFESTYLE ADJUSTMENTS

Bad habits are sometimes hard to break, but once you adopt a healthier lifestyle, you definitely won't regret that decision. Healthy habits reduce the risk of certain diseases, improve your physical appearance, and improve your mental health. They can also give your energy level a much-needed boost.

You won't necessarily change your mindset or behavior overnight, so it is important to be patient and take one day at a time. But it does boil down to making small changes that begin to add up over time.

Ways to Deal With Stress

To deal with stress, you will want to avoid:

- Sugar
- Dairy, especially casein found in cow's milk

- Grains, such as gluten and phytic acid
- GMO foods with pesticides

Experiencing what I call *toxic emotions* is not a live-or-die level of danger, but it can be very stressful. Once toxic emotions grow within you, your brain turns on that fight-or-flight system and starts to send signals to your entire body so it can focus on how to protect itself from the harm of your toxic emotions. Here are some ways to help you take the edge off your fight-or-flight system.

The moment those toxic emotions turn on, the stress switch on your mind turns on too. When you experience this, I encourage you to take a moment to write down what emotion you are experiencing and where in the body you feel that emotion.

For example, it could be *fear in your throat* or *worry in your gut*. You can come back to that later.

Some people say you should face your stressor, work with it, and release it right away. But when you are deep in that chatty mind trap, it is often too late. I've found that naming emotions and figuring out where in your body you are feeling them is the first healthy process to slow down your mind and feel the emotions fully.

Here are some methods to try working with these emotions:

Laughter

We all know it's beneficial, but science shows that laughter helps your brain create more endorphins. You can enjoy watching a TV show or YouTube video to get you in a laughing mood.

Exercising and Dancing

Since the fight-or-flight system is already ready to make you run or move faster, doing physical activity like walking, running, swimming, or dancing can help calm your adrenaline and bring the logical part of your brain back online.

Singing Out Loud

I know sometimes I feel good by singing out loud in the car. My singing in the car may not sound great. But singing out loud helps your brain create endorphins, just like laughing, and it helps calm down stress and anxiety.

Playing a Musical Instrument

Musicians know the effectiveness of this method of calming your brain, but you don't have to play beautifully. Make some noise, some sound, and align yourself with that sound while you are trying to hit a gong or pluck a guitar.

Drawing or Painting Abstract Images

You can paint your emotions.

What does anger look like?

What shape or color defines it?

You don't have to make the abstract representations of your emotions look pretty. Simply start by putting colors and shades on paper. This helps your mind relax, and it helps you feel more creative.

The reason negative emotions are toxic is that we store them in our body without dealing with them properly. With the influence of our stressed mind, we can feel so icky that we want to put emotions away and keep them down deep inside.

I encourage you to try any of the methods I mentioned to help calm your mind and body and to help you deal with toxic emotions.

Ways to Heal Your Gut

Hippocrates said, "All disease begins in the gut." Leaky gut is the root cause of the majority of health conditions across the world today.

From previous chapters, you may recall that leaky gut occurs when you get holes in the tight junctions in your gut, also known as *intestinal permeability*. In this chapter, we'll look more in depth at nutritional causes and ways to heal from leaky gut.

When the tight junctions in your intestines become damaged, certain particles like toxins, microbes, bad bacteria, and undigested proteins can leak into the bloodstream. Then an immune response starts.

This process can start at birth. Moms may be deficient in probiotics, so they are passed on to the child at birth. C-section births miss out on probiotic benefits, and other microbes are passed on to the baby. Prescription antibiotics, NSAID drugs, lack of probiotics in the diet, and inflammatory foods are all major causes of gut damage.

The following are known to cause leaky gut:

- Herbicides
- Hydrogenated oils
- Other processed oils
- Chemicals

To start healing this condition, we need to change the diet, remove triggers, and take care of lifestyle stress. Removing certain food triggers that will cause gut inflammation is crucial. In return, there are certain foods that will help repair your gut.

Here are my top six favorite foods for healing leaky gut:

- Bone broth contains proline and glycine, which help repair tight junctions in your gut. Bone broth is ideal every day and is the number one healing food for the gut.

- Probiotic-rich foods like kefir. It should be fermented 24 to 29 hours and should come from A2 cow's milk, goat's milk, or sheep's milk.

- Live-fermented vegetables such as sauerkraut or kimchi give your body the proper pH for probiotics to grow.

- Vegetables like squash, carrots, spaghetti squash, acorn squash, and butternut squash. These foods are high in nutrients and good for healthy bowel movements.

- Certain fruits like berries are high in antioxidants and help reduce inflammation in your intestine.

- Omega-3 fatty acids found in fish oil, especially from wild-caught salmon, and algal oil for vegetarians is great for healing guts.

Overall, it is a combination of removing the triggers and adding in these foods that will help repair your gut.

Implementing an Exercise Routine

Building a workout routine can be a daunting task. There are a lot of variables to account for, for example, your body, goals, schedule, lifestyle, preferences, and training experience. I will try to keep it simple here and present you with options that are helpful to your goals and lifestyles.

While getting into great shape does not require as much time in the gym as many people believe, an effective routine meets the following criteria:

- Three to five workouts per week
- Each workout is 25 to 60 minutes long
- Your routine includes resistance and cardiovascular training

Let's look at a handful of schedules and use them to build a workout routine that will enable you to reach your goals.

One of my favorite routines is the *push day, pull day, leg day* workout routine. Push-pull-leg routines have been around forever. They are simple, make biomechanical sense, and they work. On day one you perform your push exercises, such as working your chest, shoulders, and triceps. On day two you would perform your pull exercises, training your back and triceps. On day three, you would do leg exercises.

It could look like this hypothetically:

- Monday: Push day
- Tuesday: Rest
- Wednesday: Pull day
- Thursday: Rest
- Friday: Leg day

You could do Monday push, Tuesday pull, and Friday leg day, so you feel fresher come leg day.

Research indicates that total weekly training volume and intensity is more important than frequency. As long as you hit each muscle group with the right amount of heavy reps each week, doing them in one workout or three will not significantly change your results. While I am not against training each muscle group multiple times per week, I am not going to recommend it here, especially for beginners.

As you progress and become stronger, you can start to spread your routine out into four or five days. A four-day routine could look like this:

- Day one: Chest and triceps
- Day two: Back and biceps
- Day three: Shoulders
- Day four: Legs

A five-day routine could be adding your arms only instead of doing them with the chest and back days.

There are two types of primary weight-lifting exercises: compound and isolated. I recommend people focus more on compound exercises, which involve multiple major muscle groups and require the most whole-body strength and effort.

Examples of compound exercises are squats, dead lifts, bench press, and military press. If you want to build maximum muscle and strength, you want to focus on compound exercises for your workouts. You can refer to my website, docjacey.com, to look at a variety of exercises.

While cardio is not necessary for fat loss, it can help quite a bit, especially when it is high-intensity interval training. If you want muscle growth and maximum fat loss, I recommend doing three 10 to 15 minute sessions of high-intensity cardio each week in addition to your weight training. You can do your cardio on your weight-training days or your off days, but I do recommend you take at least one day of complete rest per week to help with overall recovery.

EMOTIONAL WELLNESS

Life has its occasional frustrations and disappointments. We all have and will continue to experience these testing pitfalls in our lives. How we handle these parts of our lives can greatly impact our health. Being emotionally well can help prevent unwanted health conditions. Being aware of how a situation may affect us and make us feel is important. Accept feelings of frustration, sadness, anger, or whatever they may be. Don't deny your emotions or suppress them.

I find those that have a consistent optimistic approach to life have awareness of their thoughts and feelings. They seek support when they need it. We all may need support from others at times in our lives, whether it be from a friend, family member, support group, or professional. Seeking that support is part of being emotionally well as well as expressing support for others that may need it. Emotional wellness is also tied to accepting our own mistakes and learning from them.

In my office, I ask patients to evaluate their stress and emotional wellness by asking themselves these questions:

- *Do I feel I have enough time in the day to do all the things I must do?*

- *Do I practice ways to reduce my stress?*

- *Am I maintaining balance with work, family, and other obligations?*

- *Do I have overall good concentration and memory?*

- *Am I able to make decisions without much stress?*

If they answer no to any of those questions, it's often a red flag that they may need to improve in an area of wellness.

Identifying Things That Hold You Back

In the years I have been practicing and coaching wellness, I've found that there are various habits that many of us have that can hold us back from getting exactly where we want to go.

Here are nine habits that I see most commonly:

1. **Waiting for the right moment.** There never really is a right moment, so waiting around for one is a waste of time. We need to pick a

moment, one that suits the direction we want to go, right here, right now.

2. **Needing approval from others.** We should realize that other people can't be responsible for things in our own lives. Everything that has happened in our lifetime, and everything that will happen, depends on us. So, we need to be responsible for ourselves and everything that is to come.

3. **The need to be perfect.** Don't get caught up in this. This can hold you back from simply trying things in life. Perfection does not exist, so don't let that hold you back from being the best you can be.

4. **Being too stubborn to let go.** Ideas will come and go, and so will people, businesses, colleagues, and partners. For your health to blossom, you should find a way to allow what no longer serves your best interest to leave your universe.

5. **Not willing to do something beyond your duties.**

6. **Comparing yourself to others.**

7. **Not assessing your mistakes.** Consider this quote attributed to Albert Einstein: *Insanity is doing the same thing over and over and expecting*

different results. If we are continuing to make the same mistakes again and again, it might be worth assessing.

8. **Not working on your weaknesses.**

9. **Taking life too seriously.** Life can get you down for sure, but when you feel like the world is caving in on you, remember how wonderful life is. Think about all the great people and moments that have contributed to bringing you where you are today.

I ask patients to identify these areas in themselves so we know where to begin. Most of us struggle with one or more of these issues at certain times in our lives.

Feeding Your Mind on a Regular Basis

We need to feed our mind every day.

What does this mean?

For many years, I read books and listened to audiobooks by Tony Robbins. One thing he says is that it is extremely important to feed our minds. If we don't, it is easy for negative things to enter. The news around us is now more negative than ever before. We don't have to buy a newspaper anymore; it's pretty much right in our pockets and hands. Reports of negative world events, devastating storms, mass shooting: if it bleeds, it leads.

We are drawn to these things that are catastrophic and bad. It's part of being human.

We need to make sure we feed our minds positive things every day. I encourage you to read something that you are passionate about, something you want to learn more about, or something you want to improve on. Spend at least thirty minutes a day reading material that moves you. Feed your mind through reading thirty minutes each day.

Also, listen to something positive every day. I choose to listen to Tony Robbins, Wayne Dyer, or other functional medicine practitioners I strive to be like. So, whether it's a life coach you like, or a pastor, or someone who is an expert in a field you are passionate about, listen to them. Feed your mind every day with those more positive thoughts. There are more than enough negative things that you won't have to look for, but do stand watch at the door of your mind. We need to pay more attention to what we allow ourselves to listen to and read.

Besides reading and listening to more positive things, here are some other things to help our brains and minds stay healthy and young:

- **Exercise regularly.** Exercising regularly helps the body improve brain function.

- **Play memory games or do brain exercises.** Things like chess, Sudoku, and other brain games. Also try memorizing phone numbers and doing math problems without a calculator.

- **Try new things.** Experiencing something new helps stimulate the brain. Take a different route to work. Maybe try out a new workout routine. Don't get stuck always doing the same old things.

- **Think positive thoughts.** Stress can be reduced by simply thinking of positive things.

- **Eat healthy.** Your brain needs good-quality nutrients.

- **Getting adequate quality sleep.** This is ultimately how our brain recharges itself.

Learning to Love Yourself

In order for most of us to have a good, healthy relationship with others, we need to learn to love ourselves. A lot of people continue to have health issues because they cannot feel love for parts of themselves where they continue to feel negative emotions. This is actually where we need to love ourselves most.

It is often difficult to forgive ourselves for certain things we may have done or people we may have hurt. When people continue to suffer with a lack of self-love, this can manifest itself as outward lack of love. It can be perceived as hatred. This is very toxic for that person who harbors hate. Nobody can truly start to heal until they begin to forgive, forget, and learn to love. This begins with loving themselves. We all are capable of this. We just need to try.

Start by reconnecting with the dreams you have in life. Maybe write them down on paper. Then start encouraging yourself to pursue those dreams. Tell yourself you are worth it, and you can be a light for others.

If there is an emotion you can identify that is negative, don't just ignore it. Address it as if you are a parent talking to a child.

Ask yourself:

- *What triggered this?*
- *What memories did this bring up?*
- *What pattern of reactions did this emotion create?*

This process of analyzing your emotions will help you become more aware of how your emotions and actions feed one another. Soon, you will be able to feel the toxic emotions melt away, and your negative actions and reactions also will change accordingly.

Love yourself more, and your life will become more joyful. Especially love the part of you that feels negative emotions. In fact, that is the most important part to love.

NATURAL HEALING

To begin healing our bodies naturally, we begin with being proactive. This includes adopting a healthy lifestyle. This also includes eating natural whole foods, exercising, taking natural supplements, and working to manage our stress.

A quote that I love that I use over and over again is from more than one hundred years ago by Thomas Edison. He said, "The doctor of the future will give no medicine, but will interest his patients in the care of the human frame, in diet, and in the cause and prevention of disease."

With natural healing, you are looking at the cause, and you are using a natural approach to allow the body to heal itself because we all have the innate ability to heal.

Natural Ways to Reduce Inflammation

Inflammation is part of the immune process that occurs in the body when there is some sort of insult that occurs. Inflammation is a normal part of the healing process, and it is ideal for acute situations. When the inflammation is chronic, it can become more serious and lead to many of the unwanted health conditions people suffer with. Things like autoimmune diseases commonly have a lot of systemic inflammation. Cardiovascular diseases are also associated with a lot of inflammation. Arthritis, inflammatory bowel conditions, and skin conditions all have chronic inflammation that can cause major flare-ups. Fortunately, there are many ways we can help reduce this chronic inflammation.

We like to use a combination of herbs, foods, and lifestyle habits to help patients reduce their inflammation.

Here is a list of some of my favorites herbs and spices:

- Turmeric
- Cayenne
- Ginger
- Cinnamon
- Cloves
- Sage
- Rosemary

My favorite foods for reducing inflammation are those containing Omega-3 fatty acids:

- Fish oil
- Wild-caught salmon

- Flaxseeds
- Chia seeds
- Hemp seeds
- Winter squash

As well, I recommend dark green and leafy green veggies

- Cucumber
- Zucchini
- Broccoli
- Celery
- Seaweeds

Also berries because of their high amounts of antioxidants.

Coconut products have so many benefits: coconut oil and coconut butter for the healthy fats they have. Coconut meat helps restore oxidative tissue damage, and coconut water is so good for re-hydration. Coconut is considered a superfood.

Pineapple and papaya contain beneficial enzymes that are great for digestion.

Spirulina, another superfood, is a great source of important nutrients, including essential amino acids; protein; B vitamins; and vitamins C, D, A, and E; as well as important minerals.

Some lifestyle habits that are great for helping fight inflammation are:

- Regular exercise
- Adequate sleep
- Stress management
- Detoxification
- Deep breathing
- Stretching
- Adequate hydration

In addition to the herbs, foods, and lifestyle habits, there are some things we want to avoid to reduce inflammation:

- Omega-6 fatty acids
- Processed foods and refined carbohydrates
- Gluten
- Dairy
- Over-exercising

Supplements That Help With Stress

In my office, I see many individuals who have a lot of symptoms related to chronic stress. So, I often order a test to be able to assess the amount of adrenal exhaustion a patient has. The test is called an *adrenal stress index*. With this test, I am able to see various markers and categorize what possible stage of adrenal exhaustion a person is in.

Once I have the results, I can go to work on a specific protocol that will help restore and improve adrenal function for that patient. That protocol is specific to a person's lab results, which is why I order this test before deciding what protocol to begin.

We all now grasp how effects of stress can impact our health. Many people unfortunately suffer many consequences of prolonged chronic stress, and it eventually takes a huge toll on their health. There are various natural supplements I like to use with patients who have high stress.

Without knowing an individual's adrenal stress index score, I can't begin a specific protocol, but there are great supplements that can definitely help you deal with the stress in your life. Supplements are an important piece of self-care and can help stop stress from taking over your life. These are some of my favorites that I use with patients, and I personally use a few as well.

> If you suffer from ***stress and insomnia,*** you want to use magnesium, melatonin, and valerian root. The starting dosage for magnesium is 200 milligrams. For melatonin, the starting dose would be 1 milligram. For valerian root, the starting dose is 400 milligrams.

> If a you have stress symptoms like headaches, vitamin B_6 and vitamin B_2 (riboflavin) are

effective; 25 milligrams of each are ideal. Also, feverfew, which is a headache remedy for migraines, helps — 50 milligrams.

If you have stress symptoms of pain, omega-3s are beneficial, as is curcumin. I recommend people take approximately 2–3 grams a day of omega-3s and 2 grams of curcumin.

If you suffer from stress symptoms such as anger, rage, and anxiety, try phosphorylated serine and taurine. Also, Ltheanine is helpful at 200 milligrams a day.

For stress symptoms such as poor immunity, I recommend astragalus.

For fatigue, consider rhodiola and ashwagandha; 170 milligrams of rhodiola a day is great. I like taking 500 milligrams of ashwagandha a day.

B vitamins and magnesium together help when a woman's menstrual cycle is disrupted. They help prevent the hormone decline from chronic stress.

These are the top supplements for reducing stress. *Of course, you should always consult with your physician before taking any of these supplements.*

Finding a Practitioner

If you are looking for a doctor who practices functional medicine, I can tell you that they are not always easy to find. I know, because many years ago I was on a desperate search for a practitioner and had a difficult time.

Below are tips to help you with your search that outline what to look for and what to ask when looking for a functional medicine practitioner.

Please always make sure they have the standard certifications and trainings, which is the first sign of a skilled practitioner.

1. Does the practitioner test the three body systems? A functional medicine approach to chronic illness involves testing, at minimum, the three main body systems: your hormone system, your digestive system, and your detoxification system. A skilled practitioner can help you assess what areas are working and what areas need to be corrected to rebalance your body.

2. Will the practitioner look at advanced autoimmune panels and order blood serum testing to check for deeper root causes to common problems, particularly for individuals with complex health problems?

Make sure they address the area that is your limiting factor. Great practitioners know how to find the limiting factors that are holding you back from the level of health you are seeking.

3. Practitioners should also be able to answer questions that ascertain whether one of your body's systems has crashed:

- Do you have adrenal fatigue?
- Do you have parasites?
- Are there detox problems present?

All these issues need to be understood before you recover from chronic illness plagued with inflammation, leaky gut, and gut dysbiosis.

Practitioners must also understand what it is like to be sick and get better. A skilled functional medicine practitioner who has overcome a chronic illness may prove to be beneficial. Some of the best practitioners we know are people who were sick and thus understand what it is like to crawl back from the brink of death. Don't be ashamed to ask your practitioner if they have struggled with chronic illness or digestive problems. If they have, they will be happy to share all that they have overcome.

I know this because I am one of those guys. From that place, I can understand that there are several ingredients required to get better, such as diet, supplements, and lifestyle changes. That is not to say that someone is not a good practitioner just because they haven't been sick. That is not true at all. There are great practitioners who have not been sick, but I know that all practitioners who have overcome a personal struggle can usually relate better. They may have been in your exact shoes.

In doing this as long as I have, I have experienced times when a patient is taking the supplements, exercising, and following through on dietary changes, but they are not improving. The commonality in these cases tends to be that these patients still have an emotional component that they have not fully dealt with.

If all physical components have been addressed, unprocessed emotions need to be explored in order to move forward and attain optimum health. That is why I shared the concepts of loving yourself and dealing with toxic emotions in this book. I've seen patients finally begin gaining their health once they have faced and broken through some of their old emotions.

Emotional health plays a much bigger role than most would ever think, and it is a huge part in how your body expresses health.

Conclusion

Our bodies were designed to be self-healing and self-regulating. If we give our bodies what they need and minimize the toxins and potential interferences, we will thrive and live abundantly. Health won't be gained from some new-fad diet program or cookie-cutter workout program or fasting program.

This book isn't about any of those things. I want you to see that true health begins with your decision to want to be healthy, followed by taking the steps that will lead you to wellness. It's about achieving those small wins, and each small win builds upon the whole over time.

From my years of clinical practice, I've come to realize that there are some consistencies that seem to prevent many people from having optimal health. One of the main areas is what a person believes health is to them. It's important to understand that health doesn't come from medications or surgeries.

Just because you are not diagnosed with cancer or some other disease process does not mean you are healthy. Real health comes from what you do and the lifestyle you live. How you eat, how you manage stress, your activity level, and your gut health all contribute significantly to your health.

When I see a patient who is lacking optimal health, most often, they are struggling with one or more of these issues. They may have a low-stress job and don't really feel stress is a problem for them, but they have a diet that is typical of most Americans, which lacks nutrition and is filled with toxins. Some may follow a clean and nutritious diet but their gut is not healthy. They may have leaky gut and bacterial imbalance.

Then, there are the countless patients who have adrenal exhaustion from years of stress. This causes other hormones to be out of balance, and many other symptoms begin to present themselves.

No matter the real underlying cause of symptoms, you must first acknowledge what health is for you. Then you need to make the decision to move in that direction. This does not mean you should turn your entire world upside down. You need only to decide that you want and deserve to be healthier. Once you've decided, you can assess the areas in your life that you feel need improvement.

Is it your diet? If so, begin adding healthier foods to your meals. Adding servings of vegetables with each meal will provide nutrients that may have been missing for some time. Eventually, this boost in nutrients will make the foods with little or no nutritional value a lot less desirable; they will never provide your body with what it needs.

Achieving health doesn't need to be about completely changing overnight how you eat. Making smaller changes over time will start to add up. At the same time, it is extremely important to cut your consumption of sugary, processed, and artificial foods. Those things are not really food anyway.

If your problem area is stress, which is more common in today's society, then you need to address what is causing most of that stress. Start to do things that are proven to help reduce stress:

- Go for a walk outside.
- Read a book.
- Write down your thoughts.
- Learn to accept that, no matter what, there are things in your life that you really have no control over.

That goes for all of us. I personally use prayer as one of my ways to cope with stress. I also journal when I can, and exercise helps me tremendously.

Stress is a big one, and we all must find ways to cope with and minimize stress and its negative effects. Forms of stress will always exist to some degree as long as we are alive and on this planet.

Many of us may have gut or GI problems. I am not referring only to constipation, diarrhea, or acid reflux.

Of course, those are signs that there is a problem; I am also referring to leaky gut.

I often order a food sensitivity test for patients. It's a great test because we can use blood to see which foods you are sensitive to. Once you know you have a sensitivity when you eat certain foods, you can take action to avoid those foods for a period of time to give your body a break from the inflammation caused by those foods.

It's a leaky gut that causes this process to begin, so it's important to heal the leaky gut. There are supplements I like to use for this, as well as certain foods. One of my favorite supplements for leaky gut is L-glutamine, and my favorite food is bone broth.

The next thing we need to address is the bacterial flora of the gut. We need to have an ideal amount of friendly good gut bacteria present. Many patients have too much of the bad bacteria as well as too much yeast or parasites present. This absolutely must be addressed.

The gut microbiome is so important for overall health. Probiotics are an important piece to help provide the good bacteria to your gut. This can be in the form of a probiotic capsule and also eating foods that are high in probiotics. These foods would include things like live cultured yogurts, kefir, sauerkraut, kimchi, lacto-fermented pickles, tempeh, and miso soup.

If you feel you are just not active enough, or you keep putting off that day you plan to start exercising, you are not alone. With the technology of smartphones, computers, tablets, and all the other gadgets around today, people have become extremely lazy. Being active and moving about is no longer something we feel is a priority. If you are not regularly active, start now. Don't put it off, and don't tell yourself again that you will start on Monday. Seriously, start *now* — as in, right this moment.

If you can, put this book down, and stand up. Do thirty seconds of jumping jacks. If you can't do jumping jacks, run or jog in place for thirty seconds. Do something at a high-enough intensity to get your heart rate up for a thirty-second burst. Then rest for one to two minutes until your heart rate drops and you have your breath back. Do another thirty-second burst, and then rest again. You can walk around during the rest time to keep your body moving.

I recommend doing four or five of those thirty-second bursts with one to two minutes of rest in between. You will be done in about ten minutes. This form of exercise, when done every other day, will do incredible things for your health. You think you don't have enough time to exercise, but you just found out you do!

Ten minutes, three times a week, is all you need to start burning fat and improving your health.

I want you to know you can do whatever you put your mind to. Your ability to heal and improve your health is far more powerful than you think. Start deciding for yourself that you want to be healthier and maintain that level of health.

You can do amazing things with a healthy body, mind, and spirit. It's when we really lose our health that most people start to pay attention to its importance. Don't wait until it's too late. You can definitely turn things around and improve on your current health level.

One of the people I have always looked up to and admired is Jack LaLanne. You may recall him from his juicing machines, one of which I actually happen to own. I love many of his quotes. He was more fit and healthy in his eighties than most Americans are in their twenties and thirties.

Two of my favorite Jack LaLanne quotes are:

> *There is no fountain of youth. What you put into your body is what you get out of it. You would not feed your dog a coffee and donut for breakfast followed by a cigarette. You would kill the dog.*

> *You don't get old from age. You get old from inactivity, from not believing in something.*

Another quote that I like that he used a lot is, "If man made it, don't eat it."

Please apply these principles and recommendations to your life. Apply them to those you love, as well. If you would like a consultation with me to assess your journey to health and wellness, you can always contact our office. We are here for you if you ever need us.

God bless you on your journey up the road to wellness.

My email address is drjacey@envisionwellnessonline. com. My office phone number is (402) 281-0825. Our website is envisionwellnessonline.com.

Next Steps

Be sure to visit our website: envisionwellnessonline.com.

Like us on Facebook at: facebook.com/envisionwellnesscenter/

We help patients all over the country as well as other countries outside the United States. If you are local to the Omaha, Nebraska, area, give our office a call for an appointment today at 402-281-0825. We also do phone consultations for those in other states.

Email us at healthteam@envisionwellnessonline.com.

Let us help guide you on your search for Wellness.

Resources

Anderson, Dean. "3 Simple Ways to Build Consistency." 23 Jan 2007. sparkpeople.com/resource/motivation_articles.asp?id=759

Anderson, Marlene. "When Stress Accumulates." 22 November 2011. focuswithmarlene.com/when-stress-accumulates/

B, Zoë. "8 Ways to Feed Your Brain." 23 August 2012. mindbodygreen.com/0-5913/8-Ways-to-Feed-Your-Brain.html

Beck, Julie. "Prescription Antibiotics Alter Microbial Community in Gut." 18 November 2015. geneticliteracyproject.org/2015/11/18/prescription-antibiotics-alter-microbial-community-in-gut/

Chestnut, James L. *The Wellness Prevention Paradigm.* Victoria, B.C.: TWP Press. 2011. 40–54.

Clear, James. "How to Break a Bad Habit (and Replace It with a Good One)." 13 May 2013. jamesclear.com/how-to-break-a-bad-habit

Clinical Research Society. "Exercise May Decrease the Rate of Cognitive Decline in Older Age." clinicalresearchsociety.org/exercise-may-sluggish-the-rate-of-cognitive-decline-in-older-age/

Court, Ben, and Maria Masters. "How Exercise
Affects Your Metabolism." 04 May 2015. menshealth.
com/fitness/exercise-and-metabolism

Fitday Editor. "The Importance of Working Out with
Consistency." fitday.com/fitness-articles/fitness/
exercises/the-importance-of-working-out-with-
consistency.html

Foley, Brian. "Early Detection of Brain Impairment:
Key to Long Term Health." Health and Wellness
Center, 7 Dec 2013. youralternativedoctor.com/early-
detection-of-brain-degeneration-key-to-long-term-
health/

Frey, Malia. "What Is Metabolism and How Do I
Change It?" 01 Nov. 2015. verywell.com/what-is-
metabolism-and-how-do-i-change-it-3495537

Godman, Heidi. "Regular Exercise Changes the
Brain to Improve Memory, Thinking Skills." Harvard
Health Blog, 09 April 2014. health.harvard.edu/blog/
regular-exercise-changes-brain-improve-memory-
thinking-skills-201404097110

Grisanti, Ronald. "Leaky Gut: Can This Be
Destroying Your Health?" FMU. 12 Sept 2016.
functionalmedicineuniversity.com/public/Leaky-
Gut.cfm

Hitti, Miranda. "Exercise Prevents Arthritis Disability." Jan 2016. webmd.com/arthritis/news/20060106/exercise-prevents-arthritis-disability

"How to Know You Have Leaky Gut: Signs and Symptoms of Leaky Gut." 13 Sept 2016. myleakygutsyndrome.com/how-to-know-you-have-leaky-gut-signs-and-symptoms-of-leaky-gut/

Hunnewell, Jennie. "Gastrointestinal Function." Oklahoma City: OKC - H-MD. 01 Sept 2016 h-md.com/gastrointestinal-function/

Kalish, Daniel. *The Kalish Method*. Richard Kalish Publishing. 2012. 32–38.

Katsuta, Keiko. "5 Fun Ways to Deal with Toxic Emotions and Thoughts." 28 Dec 2015. aha-now.com/deal-toxic-emotions-thoughts/

Kerr, Michael, and Jacquelyn Cafasso. "Malabsorption Syndrome." 27 July 2016. healthline.com/health/malabsorption

Lam, Michael. *Adrenal Fatigue Syndrome*. Loma Linda, CA: Adrenal Institute Press. 2012. 51–59.

Marksteiner, *Kelsey*. "Is Stress Wrecking Your Gut?" 08 May 2014. robbwolf.com/2014/05/08/stress-wrecking-gut/

Mathews, Michael. "The Definitive Guide on How to Build a Workout Routine." musclelustihood.com/how-to-build-a-workout-routine/index.htm

Mayo Clinic. "Exercise: 7 Benefits of Regular Physical Activity." mayoclinic.org/healthy-lifestyle/fitness/in-depth/exercise/art-20048389?

Medder, Ben. "Humans Are Meant to Move." 20 Sept 2016. benmedder.com/movement/

Melone, Sara. "How Does Exercise Improve Digestion?" healthyliving.azcentral.com/exercise-improve-digestion-4714.html

Mercola, Joseph. "Chronic Stress Doesn't Stay in Your Head." 12 March 2105. articles.mercola.com/sites/articles/archive/2015/03/12/chronic-stress.aspx

Mercola, Joseph. "The Minimum Amount of Exercise You Really Need." 03 April 2015. fitness.mercola.com/sites/fitness/archive/2015/04/03/recommended-amount-exercise.aspx.

Mercola, Joseph. "Processed Foods Hurt Your Immune System and Gut Health." 16 June 2014. articles.mercola.com/sites/articles/archive/2014/07/16/processed-foods-immune-system-gut-health.aspx

Mercola, Joseph. "Regular Exercise Reduces Large Number of Health Risks" 09 Dec 2010. fitness. mercola.com/sites/fitness/archive/2010/12/09/ regular-exercise-reduces-large-number-of-health-risks.aspx

Mercola, Joseph. "Top 10 Reasons to Strength Train" 18 Nov 2011. fitness.mercola.com/sites/fitness/ archive/2011/11/18/strength-train-reasons.aspx

Morris, Megan. "Dysbiosis." 08 Sept 2016. therootofhealth.com/dysbiosis/

O'Connell, Danielle. "Exercise for Detox." 16 Aug 2010. livestrong.com/article/206993-exercise-for-detox/

Omega Institute for Holistic Studies. "What Does Wellness Mean to You?" *Omega*. 03 April 2015. eomega.org/article/what-does-wellness-mean-to-you, 20 August 2016

Peloguin, Andrew. "How Exercise Affects Your Metabolism." fitday.com/fitness-articles/fitness/ how-exercise-affects-your-metabolism.html

Perlmutter, David. "NSAIDs, the Gut, and Inflammation." 04 Sept 2016. drperlmutter.com/ nsaids-gut-inflammation/

Reasoner, Jordan. "How to Find a Trusted Functional Medicine Practitioner." scdlifestyle.com/2014/11/how-to-find-a-trusted-functional-medicine-practitionSCIAer/

SJ Functional Medicine. "Functions of the Gastrointestinal System." 2017. sanjosefuncmed.com/successful-aging-part-8a-functions-gastrointestinal-system/

About the Author

Dr. Jacey Folkers is a wellness expert on lifelong optimized living. For the past seventeen years, he has created and implemented breakthrough lifestyle programs for individuals. He has worked for many years with all types of patients, including professional athletes, and is an engaging public speaker who has educated thousands.

His passion is for healthy living and educating others to help them reach their own health goals. He continues to speak at his regular health seminars, corporate workshops, lunch-and-learn events, and private classes.

He has been featured on numerous local talk shows as an advocate for gaining and preserving wellness through natural means and lifestyle enrichment, rather than disease management. His professional education includes doctor of chiropractic, functional wellness, nutrition, and fitness.

He is also president and clinical director of the Envision Wellness Center and founder of Midwest Integrative Health.